INSTITUTIONAL ECONOMICS

INSTITUTIONAL

ECONOMICS

Veblen, Commons, and Mitchell Reconsidered

A SERIES OF LECTURES BY
Joseph Dorfman, C. E. Ayres, Neil W.
Chamberlain, Simon Kuznets, R. A. Gordon

University of California Press 1963
BERKELEY AND LOS ANGELES

UNIVERSITY OF CALIFORNIA PRESS
BERKELEY AND LOS ANGELES, CALIFORNIA

CAMBRIDGE UNIVERSITY PRESS
LONDON, ENGLAND

Foreword

Institutional economics was once described by the late Edwin E. Witte as "a method of studying economic phenomena rather than a connected body of thought expressing the 'timeless and placeless laws' which govern what Frank Knight referred to as 'the economic calculus of individual preference.' " It represents a distinctly American contribution to economic theory, and in this respect is closely related to the movements of pragmatism in philosophy and, to a somewhat lesser degree, sociological jurisprudence in law.

Institutional economists have never confined themselves to the classical economic theory of value and distribution. They have freely disregarded the arbitrary lines of demarcation between the academic disciplines and have stressed so-called non-economic factors in their analysis of economic problems, especially those having to do with labor. They have also insisted that the first condition of sound theory is that it be based on thorough knowledge of relevant facts, and they have developed a methodology which stresses the systematic gathering and rigorous analysis of these data.

Institutional economics has provided much of the information and method upon which our present ways of handling and studying industrial relations problems are based. Its importance in the contemporary context is attested by the eminence of the five contributors to this volume, four of whom journeyed considerable distances to deliver their lectures personally at the University of California, Los Angeles. Each of the five is not only a specialist on one or more of the founders of institutional theory, but is also a major figure in the field of economics.

The three men whose work is the principal subject of this book—Thorstein Veblen, John R. Commons, and Wesley C. Mitchell—are generally regarded as the founders of the institutional school in economics. The only other recognized contender for that title is Charles Horton Cooley, who is mentioned in Professor Dorfman's essay. Many other notable figures, however, have followed in their footsteps, among them Arthur J. Altmeyer, Mordecai Ezekiel, Walton H. Hamilton, Robert F. Hoxie, William M. Leiserson, Isador Lubin, Selig Perlman, Sumner Slichter, and Edwin E. Witte. These men and many others have made important contributions to the field of industrial relations. In sponsoring this series of lectures and publishing them in book form, the Institute of Industrial Relations, University of California, Los Angeles, honors the work of all those who have developed the fundamental principles and methods of institutional economics and have thereby illuminated and helped to resolve some of the most critical social issues of our time.

The Institute wishes to express its special thanks to the five distinguished authors of this volume—Joseph Dorfman, C. E. Ayres, Neil W. Chamberlain, Simon Kuznets, and R. A. Gordon—whose individual essays represent major contributions to the literature of institutional economics.

BENJAMIN AARON, *Director*
Institute of Industrial Relations

Contents

ONE

The Background of

Institutional Economics

The University of California is a most appropriate sponsor of a series of lectures on institutionalism.* It is natural that this university as well as its sister institutions on the Pacific Coast, being newer and less traditionbound, should have been receptive to the revolutionary implications of institutional economics. Indeed, this institution provided a stimulating atmosphere for scholars of the movement to adapt, transform, and broaden economic theory to fit the needs of the twentieth century. Looking back, it is obvious that the economic doctrines laid down during the early stages of the Industrial Revolution in England had become inadequate in the years following the American Civil War.

For two of the three founders of institutionalism—Thorstein B. Veblen, John R. Commons, and Wesley C. Mitchell—whose contributions will be discussed by subsequent lecturers, the University of California was an important part of the background. Mitchell did his most creative work during his decade at Berkeley. It was there

---

* I wish to thank my friend and former student Arthur Bekenstein for assistance in the preparation of this paper.

that he began a vast imaginative study of the development and functioning of the money economy. It was there that he completed the segment of the project published by the University of California Press under the title *Business Cycles* (1913). This massive tome is a milestone in the growth of quantitative economic research. Perhaps as important as the pioneering analysis itself was its role in bringing to this type of endeavor an acceptance and respect hitherto not afforded by influential opinion. As a result, a growing stream of the nation's best talent has been channeled into what has become a new major field in economics. Although I have spent most of my working years in the East, I was reared in the West; and since a Westerner always retains a natural sympathy for the West, it may be regional patriotism that induces me to contend that Mitchell's landmark book also represented the first flowering of intellectual achievements in the social sciences, which have become so characteristic of the great universities of the West.

During his stay in Berkeley, Mitchell also published the studies which remain the authoritative work on one of the most critical periods in American financial history—the greenback period. These were *A History of Greenbacks* (1903) and *Gold, Prices, and Wages under the Greenback Standard* (1908). Particularly noteworthy was his elaboration of the principle that prices should and could be classified into groups and that the time series revealed consistent leads and lags between these groups. In this idea lay the basis for our current use of price changes as indicators for predicting changes in the level of business activity.

Another of his important contributions during the California period was the essay, "The Backward Art of Spending Money," which, despite the deceptive blandness of phrasing so typical of him, questioned in the profoundest terms a mainstay of orthodox economics—namely, the assumption of the rationality and sovereignty of the consumer. In that essay he searchingly pointed out that the "capacities and facilities [of consumers] are most sketchy relative to the requirements of their exacting task as purchasers." It has been well said by J. M. Clark that "it is difficult to imagine a more distinguished analysis of this theme, and remarkably few allowances need to be made for the passage of forty-nine years since it was written." [1]

It is also of interest that while Mitchell was portraying the merits of institutionalism or, as he then called it, the "genetic and realistic" type of economic theory, in his course in Advanced Economics in 1907, he used the problem of wages as the illustration. He concluded the analysis by saying:

Such [a] discussion [of wages] would probably differ from the conventional sort most conspicuously in that
   (1) It would be realistic—descriptive analysis.
   (2) It would treat [the] wages-problem as part of an unceasing business process [and] not [as] a single bargain between two men.
   (3) It would not assume that both parties had complete freedom of choice or complete knowledge of [the] situation, or were fully aware of & actuated only by their economic interests; but would seek to discover the leading psychological idiosyncrasies of both parties, & to explain their idiosyncrasies in genetic terms.

He pointedly contended later that study of the "process by which wages are fixed" should begin not, as commonly done, with "supposedly simple cases," but "with the most highly organized process because then the various factors are most likely to be explicitly expressed & in part quan-

---

[1] J. M. Clark, *Competition as a Dynamic Process* (Washington: Brookings, 1961), p. 232.

titatively formulated. I.e. take collective bargaining between some great union & some association of employers, or a government arbitration case where a full record is supplied."

Mitchell's intellectual father, Thorstein Veblen, was never on the faculty of the University of California, but while teaching at nearby Stanford University he often visited Mitchell and other friends in Berkeley and San Francisco. At the time, he gave an address at the Kosmos Club of the University of California on "The Evolution of the Scientific Point of View" (1908). This developed further the theme of his essay, "The Place of Science in Modern Civilisation" (1906). In the years since, scientists have become increasingly impressed by his prophetic insight into the need of the civilized world to adjust its cultural attitudes to the rapid changes brought about by the advances of the machine technology. During his sojourn in the West, Veblen also published his papers "On the Nature of Capital" in the *Quarterly Journal of Economics,* and was completing *The Instinct of Workmanship and the State of the Industrial Arts.* Both works stress, as do all of Veblen's major studies, the strategic importance of technological advance—more broadly, scientific research—in economic growth. Most economists today have accepted this position so unquestioningly that it is regarded almost as a matter of self-evident common sense. As the scholarly former chairman of the Research Council of the RAND Corporation, C. J. Hitch, put it last year: "By far the larger part of the increase in productivity in western economies is accounted for by the baby we used to throw out with the bath water when 'for the sake of simplicity' we assumed a constant state of the technological art." [2]

---

[2] C. J. Hitch, "The Uses of Economics," in *Research for Public Policy* (Washington: Brookings, 1961), p. 99.

I might note in passing that although the term "leisure class" is today inextricably interwoven with Veblen's name, it has much earlier West Coast antecedents. I was amused on my last visit here in 1949 to discover in the records of the Berkeley Club an item written long before Veblen began his work but which I am almost certain he never saw. The entry referred to a paper entitled "The Value of a Leisure Class." I was unable to find any account of this paper, which was given in 1876, but I discovered an intriguing statement on the subject by a member of the club, Caspar T. Hopkins.[3] Veblen would not, I think, have accepted Hopkins's view that a leisure class was essential to build up the social sciences, but he would have substantially agreed with Hopkins's description of the life of the wealthy in California: "There is an abundance of first rate talent here, but no time for theorizing on social science topics, still less for the observation and collection of facts. Speculation-excitement, money getting, monopolize the time of our people with an exigence proportional to their ability—and if they do not break down ere their fortunes are secured, they go East or to Europe to enjoy them."

A number of brilliant graduates of this university participated in the subsequent development of institutionalism, particularly in applying its tools and way of thinking to new and wider areas. One was H. W. Stuart, who went

---

[3] Hopkins was prominent in the political and business affairs of the state. He zealously promoted the study of the social sciences and occasionally lectured at the university.

"The Berkeley Club . . . is a private debating society in Oakland, whose members are limited to thirty, and to which none but college-bred men are eligible, who are capable of thinking, talking, and writing to good purpose. The ablest professors in the University constitute about half the members; the others are lawyers, doctors, scientists, etc." "The California Recollections of Caspar T. Hopkins," *California Historical Society Quarterly*, December 1948, p. 340.

from this university to a fellowship at the University of
Chicago, where, like Mitchell, he was impressed not only
by Veblen but by that fellow spirit, John Dewey. When
Stuart formally shifted to philosophy for the Ph.D., he by
no means dropped his interest in economics. On the contrary, he enriched it by his doctoral dissertation, *Valuation
as a Logical Process,* and his subsequent essay, "The Phases
of the Economic Interest," [4] both of which can still be read
with profit, especially by those interested in welfare economics and the limitations of marginal utility analysis.
The friendship between Mitchell and Stuart that began at
Chicago ripened during the period when Mitchell was at
Berkeley and Stuart was at Stanford. Their common interest in economic psychology doubtless helped clarify Mitchell's conception of the institutional character of the money
economy and its "technical exigencies" which create business cycles.

Another prominent son of the university was the pas-
sionate Carleton H. Parker, who saluted Veblen as a guide.
He taught first at his alma mater and then at the neigh-
boring University of Washington, where he was also Dean
of the School of Business Administration. He pioneered in
bringing to the attention of economists and business leaders the need for a knowledge of the involved psychological
forces present in industrial relations.

Still another famous alumnus of this university, A. C.
Miller, doubtless best known to you as a member of the
original Federal Reserve Board, taught both Veblen and
Mitchell. Later, while Flood Professor of Political Economy and Commerce, he was instrumental in bringing
Mitchell to the California faculty. Despite his more con-
servative views, he had a large share of that wonderful

---

[4] H. W. Stuart, "The Phases of the Economic Interest," in John Dewey
et al., Creative Intelligence: Essays in the Pragmatic Attitude (New York:
Holt, 1917), pp. 282–353.

western-oriented belief in intellectual freedom, which allowed him to admire Veblen as "a brilliant and dispassionate critic of the prevailing position of economics." [5]

So much for the sons. How about the daughters of the University of California? Sarah McLean Hardy (later Mrs. Warren Gregory), like Stuart, received her Ph.D. at Chicago but was a graduate of this university. She inspired Veblen and Mitchell to their greatest efforts. She was their Egeria, a counselor and critic. She had the advantage of being the salon woman *par excellence* while at the same time meeting them on their own footing as an expert in that most elusive of subjects, monetary theory. Thus she could pierce the subtlety of *The Theory of the Leisure Class* to Veblen's admiration, and she could discuss with Mitchell the most intricate points that went into *Business Cycles*.

Some of you may recall Jessica B. Peixotto, a colleague and intellectual co-worker of Mitchell. She was a shrewd, skilled investigator, with gifts much like his. Her aid, as well as that of Mrs. Gregory, is acknowledged in *Business Cycles*. Among the western women we must include Theresa McMahon, a graduate and long-time teacher of the University of Washington. She was a student and friend of the third member of the great triumvirate of institutionalists, John R. Commons.

Jessica B. Peixotto, Theresa McMahon, Carleton H. Parker, and another western colleague of Mitchell and fellow institutionalist, Solomon Blum, helped to create the intellectual climate that gave birth to the Institute under whose auspices we are meeting.

I have found no direct personal connection between the University of California and John R. Commons, but certainly this Institute is intellectually related and indebted

---

[5] A. C. Miller, "Economic Science in the Nineteenth Century," in *Congress of Arts and Science, Universal Exposition, St. Louis, 1904*, ed. by H. J. Rogers (Boston: Houghton Mifflin, 1906), Vol. VII, p. 22.

to the Commons tradition. Could anyone knowing the
principles followed in the work here, namely, its devotion
to using the tools of investigation as a means of developing
and testing public policy, its cutting across the conventional boundary lines of the social sciences, and its recognition of group or collective action, as well as individual
behavior, doubt that this Institute is a living part of the
movement that had Commons as its fountainhead?

Let me turn to my main task, the setting of institutionalism. No single lecture could do justice to this subject, for
the leaders explored an enormous area of the social sciences, and their positive achievement constitutes one of
the most influential and distinctively American contributions to economic thought. Furthermore, it is not economics in the usual sense, but a slice of the whole development of civilization in the United States since the end of
the Civil War. I view this type of economics as both an
answer to the older demand for, and a continuation of, a
new economics.

But it was much more than this, for it gave us a whole
new way of thinking about economic problems. To appreciate how important this departure was, imagine what current economics would be without the impact upon our
times of Veblen's anthropological approach, and the resulting disconcerting insights which make him, in the
words of J. M. Clark, "one of the great formative influences in the transformation of our economic thought in the
past half century." [6] Imagine economics without the understanding of living institutions which we have received
as a legacy from the historico-legal approach of Commons
and the many students who have followed in his footsteps.
Imagine a treatment of the problem of inflation and reces-

---

[6] J. M. Clark, review of *Thorstein Veblen: A Critical Reappraisal*, in
Political Science Quarterly, September 1959, p. 429.

sion without the vast growth of quantitative work now available thanks to Mitchell's example and inspiration.

The fathers of institutionalism were intellectual rebels, but they were not critics from the outside with little mastery of the discipline. They were thoroughly trained in traditional economic doctrine, but were dissatisfied with its limitations and rigidities. Consequently, their rebellion never took the form of attempts to sweep away the existing science; their efforts were directed to fashioning new forms of analysis and transforming old tools into new instruments, requisite to the demands of the twentieth century. In so doing, they extended the boundaries of the science both in depth and in range. They showed a sensitivity to all the tendencies in their own and related fields. They were deeply interested in the philosophy of pragmatism and its close companion, functional psychology (later called behaviorism) ; in the newly growing disciplines, such as sociology and anthropology; in the recognition of the relationship of legal institutions to economics; and in the emphasis on more exact empirical inquiry, especially in the use of historical documents and in the systematic collection of statistical data and the development of statistical techniques. In economic theory, the institutionalists took account of such developments as the German historical school and the marginal utility and neoclassical schools. All three founders knew Marx's work and appreciated his concern with the trend of institutional change. To the institutionalists, who adhered to a philosophy which we now loosely characterize as pragmatism, the basic limitation of Marx was his Hegelian metaphysics and rigid Ricardian economics. In fact, the view of Marx and his disciples as "pre-Darwinian"—to use Veblen's term—is a major negative characteristic of institutionalists and serves to differentiate them from most of the critics of the dominant economics.

Institutionalism is a product of the last third of the nine-teenth century. The economic problems of this post-Civil War period placed a heavy strain on the dominant laissez-faire tradition inherited from the Jacksonian era. The flowering of Jeffersonian egalitarianism occurred during the Jacksonian period. Its advocates attacked the perqui-sites and privileges of feudal, aristocratic society, which endowed the idle few at the expense of the industrious many. In their view these privileges, created by law, were the source of hated monopoly. Without them, it was be-lieved, there could not arise the obstinate, shocking con-trasts between wealth and poverty that must spell the doom of republican government. The widespread diffu-sion of property was the safeguard of democratic society. The principle of free competition, to this way of thinking, was simply the application of the moral duty of self-assertion to man's economic activity.

The post-Civil War era was a period of tremendous eco-nomic growth accompanied by radical advances in tech-nology and industrial organization. It was the era of the great captains of industry. It was the age of the spread and accelerated development of such far-reaching social and mechanical inventions as the corporation, the factory, the telegraph, the telephone, and that most potent instrument of America's first mighty industrial revolution, the rail-road. It saw the opening of the "great American desert," with its vast public lands, and the exploitation of the natural resources of the West, the nation's last geographi-cal frontier. There were enormous opportunities not only for the natives but for the flood of immigrants attracted by the prospects of freedom from oppression and the promise of wealth. The creators of the liberalism of the Jefferson-Jackson era had not envisaged the rise and domination of the new instruments and institutions, and, of course, could not have been expected to provide the nation with the means for coping with the emerging problems. Along with the magnificent material achievements of the 1870's and 1880's came a whole new range of economic and social problems. There were massive strikes, at times almost threatening civil war; there were the ills of growing urbanization, such as slums; there were widespread buccaneering practices of corporations; there was the reckless disposal of the western public lands and their natural resources; there was the terrifying corruption in politics; there was a breakdown of monetary standards in peacetime. Worst of all, there was the terror of long periods of severe business depression with accompanying nationwide unemployment.

The economists who enjoyed the highest respect and distinction were, on the whole, strong spokesmen of the dominant views of the business community. They generally attributed the ugly by-products of economic growth to inherent defects in human nature or state intervention. Typical of this group was the influential J. Laurence Laughlin, a teacher of both Veblen and Mitchell. He believed that the changing facts of economic life had as yet not altered any basic principle of political economy. All that was needed, he explained in 1884, was to substitute for the old British illustrations fresh American ones which could be "found everywhere about us in our big country." [7]

Similarly, the most popular textbook writer, A. L. Perry of Williams College, dismissed out of hand the common proposals for remedying low wages, such as trade unions, a legal minimum wage, or concentrated pressure of public opinion on employers, because these panaceas violated the axiom that naturally fixed wages, namely, the wage-fund theory. The rate of wages was a matter of simple arithme-

---

[7] J. Laurence Laughlin to Edward Atkinson, December 23, 1884, in Atkinson Papers, Massachusetts Historical Society.

tic. "If we call . . . [the] portion of capital [devoted to the payment of wages] . . . a dividend, and the number of laborers a divisor, the quotient will be the general average rate of wages at that time and place. This principle invariably determines the current rate of wages in any country." [8]

As for depressions or, as they were then called, "commercial crises," Horace White, the American counterpart of Walter Bagehot, held in 1883 that they could not be explained by the heretical theory of general overproduction, but by speculation and maladjustments. To eliminate crises would require that mankind "keep out of debt. . . . Civilization [however] is so interlaced with the credit system that it is idle to talk of abolishing it. The interests of mankind require that it should continue, even at the cost of its abuses and of the miseries of an occasional crisis." Something, he thought, could be done to mitigate the evil, especially money panics, "by diffusing correct knowledge of the principles underlying these painful phenomena. . . . At present, it must be admitted that economists themselves are not sufficiently agreed upon the fundamental principles of commercial crises to command strict attention from the unprofessional classes." This same general view was succinctly put by Laughlin: "In years of depression we hear most of the irrational theories of a general over-production in all industries. It is only an ill-adjusted production which has been caused by the ruinous speculation; and as soon as the adjustment is properly made, people go on producing far more than in the years when they talked of over-production." [9]

---

[8] A. L. Perry, *Elements of Political Economy* (New York: Scribner, 1868) , p. 123.

[9] Horace White, "Commercial Crises," in *Cyclopaedia of Political Science, Political Economy, and the Political History of the United States,* ed. by J. J. Lalor (Chicago: Rand, McNally, 1882) , Vol. I, p. 530; J. Laurence Laughlin, *The Elements of Political Economy* (New York: American Book Co., 1887) , 1896 ed., p. 157.

A common proposed remedy was public works, but prevailing economic opinion held that it was mischievous and futile. This view was clearly expressed in 1874 by the influential Congressman (later President) James A. Garfield, who had considerable knowledge of economics. He held that the true remedy for the finances in the present crisis was "economy and retrenchment, until business restored itself." It was not a proper function of the national government "to find employment for people." For example, suppose the government spent such an enormous sum as $100,000,000 for the purpose. "We should be taxing forty millions of people to keep a few thousand employed." [10]

In general, dominant economics presented the picture of narrow practicality and what critics called a "refined scholasticism" backed by all the forces of intellectual and religious conservatism.

At the same time, however, there was increasing collective action, both by the state and by voluntary associations, to curb "excesses of egoism." The increase of state intervention was such that the shrewd British observer of American affairs, James Bryce, was struck in 1886 by "the general acceptance of the Laissez Faire theory & its practical neglect." [11] The period witnessed the growth of commissions for the regulation of railroads, first by the states and then, with the establishment of the Interstate Commerce Commission (1887), by the federal government. It saw states enact antimonopoly statutes and Congress pass in 1890 the Sherman Anti-Trust Act. It saw the creation of

---

[10] James A. Garfield to B. A. Hinsdale, December 8, 1874, in *Garfield-Hinsdale Letters*, ed. by Mary L. Hinsdale (Ann Arbor: University of Michigan Press, 1949), p. 300; letter from Garfield, December 5, 1874, quoted in T. C. Smith, *The Life and Letters of James Abram Garfield* (New Haven: Yale University Press, 1925), Vol. I, p. 517.

[11] James Bryce to Albert Shaw, January 3, 1886, in Shaw Papers, New York City Public Library.

state bureaus of labor statistics and, in 1884, the federal Bureau of Labor, established to investigate labor conditions. It witnessed the emergence of a permanent national trade-union movement to protect the interests of the wage earner. It saw, too, the rise of powerful organizations of farmers and the proliferation of employer and trade associations.

The period also saw the launching of the social settlement idea, inspired largely by the example of Toynbee Hall in Whitechapel, London, which was established in 1885. Shortly afterwards, the Neighborhood Guild was formed in the New York slums, and in 1889 came the most famous settlement house, Jane Addams's Hull House in Chicago.

In some respects the most significant development was the establishment by Congress of the Geological Survey in 1879 to undertake "the classification of public lands and examination of the geological structure, mineral resources, and products of the national domain." Most noteworthy was the position of Congressman Abram S. Hewitt, himself a wealthy iron and steel magnate, who assumed the task of piloting the bill through the House of Representatives. He agreed that the measure was essential to safeguard the future lest the nation's birthright "should be mortgaged to grasping corporations or to overpowering capitalists." [12]

The legislation marked the beginning of effective national planning of the use of natural resources by centralizing the work in a permanent body of scientists and thus ending the practice of casual, temporary, and often competing government surveys. Major John Wesley Powell, the guiding genius of the Geological Survey, held that gov-

---

[12] Abram S. Hewitt, "Consolidating the Western Surveys," 1879, reprinted in his *Selected Writings*, ed. by Allan Nevins (New York: Columbia University Press, 1937) , p. 210.

ernment should promote the welfare of the people by providing for "investigation in those fields most vitally affecting the great industries in which the people engage."
It should benefit agriculture as well as mining industries.
Under his direction, the Geological Survey devoted much
effort to reducing floods like those of the Mississippi, and
to devising conditions under which "the great arid regions
may be economically fertilized by irrigation" and the coast
marshes and interior swamps drained.[13] The Geological
Survey supplied the talent that so successfully carried out
the Reclamation Act of 1902, and was the spiritual father
of the TVA and similar projects of our day.

Spearheading the intellectual advance was the triumph
of Darwinian evolution, which was defined as the "doctrine of slow and minute changes, each brought about by
natural forces, each surviving and perpetuating itself in
proportion as it is adapted to the environment of the or-
ganism in which it takes place." In the United States,
however, as well as in the land of its birth, the principle
was applied in the social sciences in two radically different ways. In both, social evolution was conceived of as the
process of advance, but in the original form, presented by
Herbert Spencer in England and by his counterpart, William Graham Sumner, in the United States, evolution as
the survival of the fittest entailed "the defeat of the many"
and the prodigal waste of "life and the possibilities of
life." [14] Spencer asserted, in *Social Statics* (1872 edition),
"that the poverty of the incapable, the distresses that come

---

[13] J. W. Powell to W. B. Allison, February 26, 1886, in *Joint Commission
to Consider the Present Organization of the Signal Service, the Geological
Survey, Coast and Geodetic Survey, and the Hydrographic Office of the
Navy Department with a View to Secure Greater Efficiency and Economy
of Administration of the Public Service in Said Bureaus*, 49th Cong., 1st
Sess., S. Misc. Doc. 82, p. 1079.

[14] Charles Beard, *The Reformation of the Sixteenth Century* (London:
Williams and Norgate, 1883), pp. 392–394.

upon the imprudent, the starvation of the idle, and those shoulderings aside of the weak by the strong, which leave so many 'in shallows and in miseries,' are the decrees of a large far-seeing benevolence." This conclusion was seized upon by the stanchest advocates of dominant extreme laissez-faire economics as reinforcing their position.[15]

Later a different view grew increasingly popular, a view most succinctly presented by the dean of American sociologists, Lester Frank Ward, then employed as a paleontologist by the Geological Survey. In *The Psychic Factors of Civilization* (1892) he argued that Darwinian natural selection had produced an intelligent being, man, capable of consciously altering his environment. The results of such actions, Ward continued, are denounced by laissez-faire thinkers as artificial and disruptive of progress, but "If the organization and improvement of government and of all other human institutions as well as the operation of the various civilizing agencies of mankind are normal products of evolution, and have taken place under the operation of natural laws, made possible only through the existence of the intellectual faculty of man, . . . what is there in the world that can be called artificial?" Since these so-called artificial decisions were really a part of the course of natural selection, it was the first duty of society, held Ward in *Dynamic Sociology* (1883), to educate the mass so as to "elaborate and expand the reasoning powers of man." For, he declared, "increase of wisdom can alone realize higher degrees of social development."

---

[15] Bryce complained that the real worth of the laissez-faire doctrine had suffered in England from the "extreme and . . . unreasonable way in which H. Spencer has presented it. He makes it seem ridiculous . . . [T]he best way to present the doctrine is to say that there is a certain presumption in favor of laissez faire sufficient to throw the onus of proof on any one proposing state action." Such action would be justified where "private action will not do what is needed" and "public or state action will [not] involve incidental mischiefs greater than that it is intended to remove." Bryce to Albert Shaw, January 3, 1886, in Shaw Papers.

Earlier, in 1877, while an employee of the Bureau of Statistics of the Department of the Treasury, Ward had urged the creation of a central bureau of statistics to make possible scientific lawmaking. He proposed that "every movement of whatever nature, going on in the country" should be reported regularly to a "Central Office or Bureau," which would systematize the data and then transmit them periodically to Congress. Placing the census in this office would end the chaotic current procedure of establishing hastily a new, temporary census organization every ten years.[16]

Ward's chief in the Geological Survey, Major Powell, envisaged the developing economy as leading to an expansion of "the operative functions" of government, on the one hand, and of corporations by private individuals, on the other. Both were essential to achieve the efficiency of the "steadily increasing division of labor, and the steadily increasing integration by the organization of labor." Contrary to the view of the "Spencerian philosophers," disaster would be avoided, he argued, not by refusing to legislate, but by adequate knowledge of the course of evolution, especially the study of social change, for without change there would be no development.[17]

While heading the Geological Survey, Powell served simultaneously as the first Director of the Bureau of American Ethnology of the Smithsonian Institution, where he did much to encourage the infant science of anthropology. Many of the findings in the new field helped to cast further doubts on the validity of the so-called immutable, universal maxims of traditional economics. During this period appeared such influential studies as those by the father of

---

[16] L. F. Ward, "The Way to Scientific Law Making," 1877, reprinted in his *Glimpses of the Cosmos* (New York: Putnam, 1913), Vol. II, p. 170.

[17] Powell to W. B. Allison, February 26, 1886, in *Joint Commission . . . ,* p. 1080; [Powell,] "Ward's Dynamic Sociology," *Science,* July 27, 1883, No. 2, p. 107.

British anthropology, E. B. Tylor, and by the Americans Lewis H. Morgan and Franz Boas. Morgan, a successful Rochester corporation lawyer, believed that the institution of private property was a mighty force for the material and social progress of humanity, but he pointed out in *Ancient Society* (1877) that property was not an instinctive notion, fully fashioned from the beginning of mankind, as current vulgarized economics maintained. On the contrary, wrote Morgan, the idea of property was slowly formed in the human mind, and remained "nascent and feeble through immense periods of time. . . . Its dominance as a passion over all other passions" marked the beginning of civilization, but civilization has developed this "greed of gain" to a point where it threatens to destroy society. He exclaimed:

The outgrowth of property has been so immense, its forms so diversified, its uses so expanding and its management so intelligent in the interests of its owners, that it has become, on the part of the people, an unmanageable power. The human mind stands bewildered in the presence of its own creation. The time will come, nevertheless, when human intelligence will rise to the mastery over property, and define the relations of the state to the property it protects, as well as the obligations and the limits of the rights of its owners. The interests of society are paramount to individual interests, and the two must be brought into just and harmonious relations.[18]

At the same time, Morgan presented a strikingly modern description of economic development. He argued that inventions could be used to characterize the periods and subperiods in man's cultural evolution or progress from savagery to civilization. "The successive arts of subsistence," he said, ". . . will ultimately, from the great influence they must have exercised upon the condition of mankind,

---

[18] Lewis H. Morgan, *Ancient Society* (New York: Holt, 1877), pp. 6, 9, 527, 552.

afford the most satisfactory bases for these divisions. . . .
Each . . . will be found to cover a distinct culture, and to
represent a particular mode of life."

Of all the early leaders in anthropology, Franz Boas of-
fered an approach that was closely related to institutionalism, if indeed it might not be characterized as institutionalist anthropology. For example, in his study of the
Kwakiutl Indians he pointed out that the institution of
property gave rise to what Veblen, who was familiar with
the work, later described as conspicuous waste. According
to Boas, the method of acquiring rank and of distributing
property among these primitive Indians of British Columbia was through the potlatch, whose basic principle was
the interest-bearing investment of property. The recipient
of such a distribution at a gift feast could not refuse the
gift, although it was actually a loan which must be re-
funded with 100 per cent interest. The possession of wealth
was honorable and each Indian zealously endeavored to
amass a fortune in order to outdo a rival by means of a
potlatch.

Boas recorded that in the old days "feats of bravery
counted as well as distributions of property, but, nowadays,
as the Indians say, 'rivals fight with property only.'" The
institution, he noted, had its counterpart in modern civilized society in ostentatious expenditure of money to demonstrate superiority over detested rivals. In his preliminary
report in 1889 he concluded that the institution was
"founded on psychical causes as active in our civilized society as among the barbarous natives of British Columbia." [19]

---

[19] Franz Boas, "The Social Organization and the Secret Societies of the
Kwakiutl Indians," in *Annual Report of the Board of Regents of the
Smithsonian Institution* (1895), part 2, p. 343; Boas, "First General Report
on the Indians of British Columbia," in *Report of the Fifty-ninth Meeting
of the British Association for the Advancement of Science* (1889), p. 834.

In the field of philosophy, the period saw the decline in this country of the heretofore dominant but relatively naïve Scottish common sense philosophy. Holding that "the criterion of . . . reality is the clear testimony of consciousness," [20] its adherents appealed to the "common sense of mankind" for the justification of "fundamental truths" like the existence of God and the innate urge for private property. This philosophy was being superseded by more sophisticated types. There was serious, sustained study of the more profound, difficult idealist philosophies of Kant and Hegel. The interpretation of Kant as the philosopher of modern science, including the doctrine of evolution, attracted considerable attention to the thinker whom Veblen described as having helped to make the "aim of disinterested inquiry . . . a systematic knowledge of things as they are." [21]

More significant for our purpose was the beginning of the distinctively American philosophy of pragmatism and the allied functional psychology. This movement was initiated by Veblen's teacher, Charles Peirce, and developed by William James and John Dewey. Peirce emphasized in a series of essays on the logic of science that "the whole function of thought is to produce habits of action," that the "guiding principle[s]" of inquiry are "habits of mind," and "thought is an *action*" leading to further thought.[22] James, according to Veblen, laid down the central principle of modern psychology: the "empirical generalization that The Idea is Essentially Active"; from this it

[20] Laurens P. Hickok, *Rational Psychology* (Schenectady: Van Degobert, 1854) , p. 17.

[21] Thorstein Veblen, *An Inquiry into the Nature of Peace and the Terms of Its Perpetuation* (New York: Macmillan, 1917) , 1919 ed. (Huebsch) , p. vii.

[22] Charles S. Peirce, "The Fixation of Belief," 1877, and "How to Make Our Ideas Clear," 1878, reprinted in his *Chance, Love and Logic*, ed. by Morris R. Cohen (New York: Harcourt, Brace, 1923) , pp. 12, 43.

followed that "knowledge is inchoate action inchoately directed to an end; that all knowledge is 'functional'; that is, of the nature of use." [23]

Dewey insisted that the "mental life must be stated in active terms, those of impulse and its development instead of in passive terms, mere feelings of pleasure and pain." George H. Mead, a colleague, maintained in a summary of Dewey's celebrated article, "The Reflex Arc Concept in Psychology" (1896), that from this evolutionary standpoint of the development of action, "what we see, hear, feel, taste, and smell depends on what we are doing. . . . In our purposively organized life we inevitably come back upon previous conduct as the determining condition of what we sense at any one moment, and the so-called external stimulus is the occasion for this and not its cause." [24]

Both Peirce and Dewey were highly critical of the unrestrained pursuit of wealth as the guide for economic thinking. Peirce castigated its "greed philosophy" and predicted that "soon a flash and quick peal will shake economists quite out of their complacency." Dewey charged that dominant economic psychology recognized only one motive, "personal gain." [25]

In the realm of economics, there was considerable dissatisfaction with the state of the science not only in the

---

[23] Veblen, review of Gabriel Tarde, *Psychologie économique*, in *Journal of Political Economy*, December 1902, p. 147; Veblen, "The Place of Science in Modern Civilisation," 1906, reprinted in his *The Place of Science in Modern Civilisation and Other Essays* (New York: Huebsch, 1919), p. 5.

[24] John Dewey, review of L. F. Ward, *The Psychic Factors of Civilization*, in *Psychological Review*, July 1894, p. 405; George H. Mead, "The Definition of the Psychical," in *Decennial Publications of the University of Chicago* (Chicago: University of Chicago Press, 1903), 1st Series, Vol. 3, p. 98.

[25] Peirce, "Evolutionary Love," 1893, reprinted in *Chance, Love and Logic*, p. 270; Dewey, *Human Nature and Conduct* (New York: Holt, 1922), p. 122.

United States; it was also evident in Europe outside of
Germany. The contempt for the sterile, extremely abstract character of traditional economics was so great in
England that Sir Francis Galton, the eminent biometri-
cian, in 1877 called on the British Association for the Advancement of Science to abolish its section on Economic
Science and Statistics on the ground "that the general ver-
dict of scientific men would be that few of the subjects
treated fall within the meaning of the word scientific." [26]
Even those who admired classical economics were disturbed about its failure to cope with pressing problems.
Thus one British writer contended that, properly understood, there could be no question of the soundness of John
Stuart Mill's "well-known economic maxim, that a demand for commodities is not a demand for labor, and does
not determine either the number of laborers to be employed or the amount of their remuneration, but only the
direction in which their industry shall be exerted!" But,
he plaintively asked, "cannot . . . something be done to
relieve the paradox that it presents," especially in a period
like the current severe long depression with its mass of
idle labor and idle capital? "The one thing wanting seems
[to be] the demand for commodities." [27]
In the United States there was widespread complaint
against what Veblen's first teacher in economics, John
Bates Clark, called "antique orthodoxy." [28] A trustees'

---

[26] Francis Galton, "Considerations Adverse to the Maintenance of Section
F (Economic Science and Statistics) Submitted by Mr. Francis Galton to
the Committee Appointed by the Council . . . [of the British Association
for the Advancement of Science]," *Journal of the Statistical Society*, September 1877, p. 471.

[27] H. S. Solly, "Political Economy for Questions of the Day," *Theological
Review*, October 1879, p. 477.

[28] J. B. Clark to L. F. Ward, February 22, 1893, in Ward Papers, Brown
University Library.

committee of Columbia College declared in 1877 that, in the textbooks,

certain general principles are first assumed to be true, and are subsequently followed out to their natural conclusions by applying to them the processes of logic. That the results thus reached have failed to command general acceptance not only among the uneducated, but also with many who have made questions of Political Economy the principal study of their lives, is made evident by the widely discordant opinions which continue to be maintained by writers of ability in regard to matters which concern the very fountain springs of national prosperity. Either the truth of the assumed general principles of the theoretic writers is denied, or it is claimed that their principles are only true with so many qualifications and limitations as to render them practically useless.[29]

At the same time that academicians were questioning the relevance of the conventional manuals, the nation was being flooded with a radical literature of economic protest. Most of it was written in a highly popular form, was essentially utopian, and was produced by men who were considered outside the profession. As was previously pointed out, the fathers of institutional economics were steeped in traditional theory. Moreover, their writings, particularly those of Veblen and Commons, were certainly not presented in a popular format. Nevertheless, such tremendously popular works as Henry George's *Progress and Poverty* and Edward Bellamy's *Looking Backward* were a response to much the same social problems which, still unsolved a decade or two later, engaged the attention of the founders of institutionalism.

The discontent with the existing state of affairs from without the profession was by no means limited to the

---

[29] "Minutes of the Trustees, 1877," copy in *Columbiana*, Columbia University Libraries.

social radicals. An increasing number of enlightened, influential men envisaged the promise of America's industrialization, but were at the same time anxious to avoid the ills that disfigured England in its factory and machine age. The broadest keynote was sounded by the eminent historian and president of Cornell University, Andrew D. White. In 1880, while on leave as United States minister to Germany, he wrote: "I began, and for a long time remained faithful, in *laissez faire* ideas of political economy; but I am more & more convinced that they are inadequate to the needs of modern society. . . . What society drifts into when left entirely to *laissez faire* ideas, whether in England or America, is not altogether a very pleasing picture to me." [30]

Emphasizing the need of more exact knowledge for statesmanship was another influential Republican and man of affairs, Samuel B. Ruggles, a Columbia trustee who had labored long for the advancement of the social sciences and especially economic statistics. He had been deeply disturbed during the Civil War by the lack of adequate quantitative records of the North's resources, which he felt would convince European powers of its ultimate success. In 1863, as the official American delegate to the International Statistical Congress at Berlin, he expressed the conviction that "abstract theories and historical traditions doubtless have their use and their proper place, but statistics are the very eyes of the statesman, enabling him to survey and scan with clear but comprehensive vision, the whole structure and economy of the body politic." [31] Thus there was developing the grand design of employing pre-

[30] A. D. White to C. S. Fairchild, March 18, 1880, in Fairchild Papers, New York Historical Society.

[31] S. B. Ruggles, *Reports of Samuel B. Ruggles, Delegate to the International Statistical Congress at Berlin, on the Resources of the United States, and on a Uniform System of Weights, Measures and Coins* (Albany: Weed, Parsons, 1864) , p. 16.

cise and comprehensive statistics to serve what in modern terms is called a system of social accounting.

This leads me into a discussion of one of the most important immediate influences in the development of the various strains of institutionalism—the impact of the German historical school, using that designation in a characteristically loose form. During the seventies and eighties, for the first time a large number of students interested in the social sciences attended German universities. They came under the influence of such teachers as Adolf Wagner at Berlin, Karl Knies at Heidelberg, and Johannes Conrad at Halle. They heard vigorous and far-reaching criticisms of "the narrow definitions and rigid deductions of the orthodox English school." [32] These heresies, coming as they did from some of the most respectable voices in German intellectual life, were at first startling to the young Americans and, over the long run, were conducive to constructive ferment. Incidentally, the University of California can rightly claim to have had one of the first if not the first of the German-trained contingent in the father of its department of economics: Bernard Moses, Ph.D. Heidelberg, 1873.

The German historical school promoted the use and improvement of such powerful instruments of research as statistics and history, including comparative economic development. It also sought to give greater scope to the ethical nature of man than the classical school would permit. In fact, the historical school entertained such a broad view of the scope of economics that it was very reluctant to admit sociology as a new science, for that field was already included in its conception of political economy.

The formation of the *Verein für Sozialpolitik* (Union

---

[32] L. C. Kellogg to Albert Shaw, January 5, 1890, in Shaw Papers, New York Public Library.

for Social Politics) by the exponents of the German historical school in 1872 first called attention to the movement in Great Britain and the United States. The Union sought to promote both the industrialization of Germany and social reform along British precedents.

The secretary, Adolf Held of Bonn, was an able statistician and a leader in the campaign to meet the challenge of socialism by an advanced, comprehensive program of social security, which culminated in Bismarck's legislation of sickness, accident, and old-age insurance. His posthumous *Zwei Bücher zur Sozialen Geschichte Englands* (1881) not only made the eminent English historian of economic thought, Edwin Cannan, aware of "that close connection between the economics and politics of the Ricardian period which provides the key to many riddles," [33] but also influenced—along with Veblen's studies—Mitchell's procedure in his famous course on Current Types of Economic Theory at Columbia University. As Mitchell stated in a lecture at Harvard, "The historical school taught all of us as it taught Edwin Cannan, that there is a vital connection between the development of economic theory and the course of practical politics." [34]

American interest in the historical school was heightened by the famous address by John Kells Ingram of Trinity College, Dublin, before the British Association for the Advancement of Science in 1878, which was quickly reprinted in the United States. He was attempting to parry Galton's demand that the economics section be thrown out of the British Association on the ground that economics was not being pursued as a science. Ingram condemned

[33] Edwin Cannan, *A History of the Theories of Production and Distribution in English Political Economy from 1776 to 1848* (London: King, 1893), 3d ed., 1917, p. x.

[34] W. C. Mitchell, "On the Study of the Economic Classics," talk to the Economics Seminar at Harvard, November 2, 1925, in Mitchell Papers, Columbia University Libraries.

the extremely abstract method in current British economics and declared that the study of economic phenomena should, in accordance with the historical method, be "systematically combined with that of the other aspects of social existence." [35]

Many other scholars in the British Isles questioned accepted theory, and their works were well known on this side of the Atlantic. Most of them, like Ingram, drew on the German historical school. For example, T. E. Cliffe Leslie of Queen's College, Belfast, informed the American public that the productive superiority of modern society was due primarily to the "direction given by the course of social development to the modern intellect toward scientific discovery and practical invention." [36] A decade or so later, the major works of Fabians Sidney and Beatrice Webb appeared, notably *The History of Trade Unionism* (1894) and *Industrial Democracy* (1897). At times their approach has been compared to those of both the historical school and American institutionalism. While substantial dissimilarities are evident among these groups, it is interesting to note that both Commons and Mitchell referred to the Webbs. Mitchell praised them in particular for having shown the feasibility and fruitfulness of careful study of the actual forms of economic processes—that is, of how things happen as well as of what happens.

The emphasis on statistics by the German historical school had particular appeal to a small but important

---

[35] J. K. Ingram, "The Present Position and Prospects of Political Economy," in *Report of the Forty-eighth Meeting of the British Association for the Advancement of Science* (1878), p. 656. The address was reprinted in the United States in *The Penn Monthly*, November–December 1879, pp. 851–871, 949–964.

[36] T. E. Cliffe Leslie, "History, Economic and Legal, and the Historical Method of Investigation," in *Cyclopaedia of Political Science, Political Economy, and the Political History of the United States*, ed. by J. J. Lalor (Chicago: Carey, 1883), Vol. II, p. 455.

group which served as advisers and administrators of public policy. Their problems made them acutely aware of the dearth of relevant statistics and of techniques for systematic collection and interpretation of data. Ruggles was impressed at the meetings of the International Statistical Congress by Ernst Engel, one of the most famous economists and head of the Royal Statistical Bureau of Prussia, which was closely connected with the University of Berlin. Engel gained a great reputation for the law of consumption, now known as Engel's law, which points out that the higher the family income, the lower the proportion spent on food. Referring to the need for continuous study of family budgets, he contended that the information so derived "could enable us to predict industrial storms." [37]

A number of Americans who studied under Engel became leaders in the further development of quantitative studies in the United States. For example, Henry Carter Adams, the first statistician of the Interstate Commerce Commission (1887), devised its pivotal accounting system, which served as a model for regulation of railroads and public utilities throughout the world. The study by Roland P. Falkner of the University of Pennsylvania for the Senate Aldrich Committee, *Wholesale Prices, Wages and Transportation* (1893), with its pioneering use of index numbers on an elaborate scale, was a landmark in statistical investigation. It served for many years as the major source for the history of prices and wages in the United States and provided most of the data for Mitchell's famous studies on the greenbacks. The foremost American theoretician of statistics, Richmond Mayo-Smith, was brought to Columbia in 1877 on the ground that his training at Berlin and Heidelberg would assure the establishment of the

---

[37] R. T. Ely, *An Introduction to Political Economy* (New York: Chautauqua Press [Hunt & Eaton], 1889), p. 28.

treatment of economics on an inductive basis. Ruggles, in his report of the trustees' committee of Columbia for such an appointment, expressed the hope that the candidate would follow in the footsteps of continental European pioneers who "brought together . . . the . . . information . . . gathered by the statistical bureaus of the several governments and have sought to infer . . . the system most favorable to industrial development, the growth of national wealth, and to the fairest and most equal distribution of the rewards of labor." [38]

The two most influential statisticians in the nation expressed much sympathy for the historical school, although they had not been trained in Germany. General Francis A. Walker, who directed the United States Censuses of 1870 and 1880, at least as early as 1874 looked to the historical school to remedy the overemphasis upon the *a priori* method of orthodox economics. He complained that "I can not swallow a great many things which have been treated by the economists of the hypothetical school as axiomatic. It is high time for us to review the assumptions of political economy." [39]

Similarly, Colonel Carroll D. Wright, the first United States Commissioner of Labor (1885) and also the first economist to become president of the American Association for the Advancement of Science (Mitchell was the second), declared that the revisionist school "bids fair to include on its roll of pupils the men in all civilized lands who seek by legitimate means, and without revolution, the amelioration of unfavorable industrial and social relations." [40] As early as 1875, while chief of the Massachu-

---

[38] "Minutes of the Trustees," copy in *Columbiana*, Columbia University Libraries.

[39] Francis A. Walker to David A. Wells, June 29, 1874, in Walker Papers, Library of Congress.

[40] C. D. Wright, *The Relation of Political Economy to the Labor Question* (Boston: Williams, 1882), p. 12.

setts Bureau of Statistics of Labor, Wright introduced Engel's law of consumption in his comparative study of the
condition of workingmen. He made a fundamental advance when he showed that higher income families saved a
greater proportion of their income. This observation in
turn led to an early version of the heretical doctrine of
general overproduction. In 1878, he made the first official
estimate of unemployment in the United States, and as
United States Commissioner of Labor his first annual report was on *Industrial Depressions* (1886).

A substantial number of those who became prominent
in the profession, notably Henry Carter Adams, J. B.
Clark, Richard T. Ely, Richmond Mayo-Smith, Simon N.
Patten, and Edwin R. A. Seligman, explicitly drew some
elements of their thinking from the German historical
school. Ely, for example, included a presentation of Engel's
work on forecasting industrial storms in his *An Introduction to Political Economy* (1889), which for more than
three decades was by far the most popular textbook in the
field. The book was generally viewed as representative of
the " 'new school' of national or historical economists." [41]
His *Labor Movement in America* (1886) served as the
inspiration for the still unsurpassed institutional *History
of Labour in the United States* prepared under the direction of his student and collaborator on the textbook,
John R. Commons.

The work of Adams in the eighties best exemplifies the
adaptation and transition from the German historical
school to full-blown institutionalism in the early decades
of the twentieth century. Having first studied economics
under Francis A. Walker at Johns Hopkins, where he received his Ph.D. in 1878, Adams then spent a year in Ger-

[41] *The Reader's Guide in Economic, Social and Political Science*, ed. by
R. R. Bowker and George Iles (New York: The Society of Political Education [Putnam], 1891), p. 10.

many under the masters of the historical school. He admired the thorough German educational discipline, with its resulting fine scholarship, and the enlightened reforms of the Bismarck era, but he was disturbed by the German worship of the state and warned against the danger to liberty implicit in indiscriminate state intervention. He was also concerned about the workings of unrestrained private enterprise in the United States which, he contended, was likely, within a century, to contradict the theory of freedom. He recommended law as the best and most readily available means of counteracting these two destructive tendencies. "As the stroke of the shuttle is limited by the framework of the loom," Adams declared, "so the industrial movements of men are bound by the liberties of law and custom; and . . . the industrial weaving of society is largely determined by its legal structure. . . . Every change in law means a modification of rights; and . . . when familiar rights are changed, or, what amounts to the same thing, when new duties are imposed, the plane of action for all members of society is adjusted to a new idea." [42] Here, of course, is a seminal notion which later led to Commons's *Legal Foundations of Capitalism.*

In his widely read and influential monograph, *Relation of the State to Industrial Action* (1887), Adams maintained that government could perform two important functions in the industrial area. First, the state could raise the ethical plane or level of competition. For example, effective factory legislation would not curtail competition, but would remove serious abuses in the factory without eliminating the benefits of individual action. Second, the state could realize, for the public good, the benefits of monopoly. For this purpose, he developed the principle

---

[42] H. C. Adams, "Economics and Jurisprudence," 1886, reprinted in *Science Economic Discussion*, ed. by R. T. Ely (New York: Science Company, 1886), pp. 82, 86.

of "increasing returns" to cover industries such as railroads, which should be subject to public control.

Government control, Adams maintained, would not necessarily lead to corruption. Corruption was due to the lack of correlation between public and private functions. The inducements in private business were far greater than in the public service. Extension of the state's administrative functions, manned by an adequate, well-paid civil service, would restore harmony between the state and private service, for this would take account not only of pecuniary considerations, but also of "considerations of social distinction, the desire to exercise such powers as one may possess, and the pleasure of filling well a responsible position." [43]

Factory legislation and monopoly regulation, however, did not touch the problem of the rights and duties under which labor was performed. This led Adams in 1886 to the formulation of the case for the development of a common law of labor. Explicitly starting from Held, Adams contended that in the regime of petty industry based on tools, the ordinary rights of personal freedom secured to producers the enjoyment of the fruits of their labor. In modern large-scale industry, however, wage earners were dependent upon the owners of machines, of materials, and of places for job opportunities. Consequently, they must unite to avoid getting worsted in bargaining. Underlying their demands was the idea that they had a right of proprietorship in the industry to which they gave their skill and time. Through collective bargaining and the labor contract, Adams envisaged a crystallization of a common law of labor rights which harmonized with the development of Anglo-Saxon liberty.

---

[43] *Relation of the State to Industrial Action and Economics and Jurisprudence*, two essays, edited with an introductory essay and notes by Joseph Dorfman (New York: Columbia University Press, 1954), p. 120.

A significant indication that the future belonged to the German-trained group was its success in organizing the American Economic Association in 1885. All the officers were from this group, except the president, Francis A. Walker. Their impact was epitomized in the statement of principles of the Association, which declared that the "positive assistance" of the state was indispensable for human progress. The growth of economic science depended less on speculation and more on "the historical and statistical study of the actual conditions of economic life." The solution of the manifold problems created by the "conflict of labor and capital" required the united effort of church, state, and science. Accordingly, the "progressive development of economic conditions . . . will be met by a corresponding development of legislative policy." [44]

Today such a formulation would not be considered radical, but in the eighties it represented a tremendous departure from orthodox sentiment. In pre-Civil War days it would have been difficult to find a respectable figure who

---

[44] "Statement of Principles," *Publications of the American Economic Association,* 1st Series, Vol. I, No. 1 (1886) , pp. 35–36.

Two years before the formation of the American Economic Association, the Political Economy Club was established in 1883 largely through the efforts of J. Laurence Laughlin, who served as secretary and treasurer. It comprised not only the leading academicians, but also statesmen, businessmen, and journalists with a deep interest in economics, such as ex-Secretary of the Treasury Hugh McCulloch, Abram S. Hewitt, Charles Francis Adams, Edward A. Atkinson, David Ames Wells, Henry Villard, Carl Schurz, Horace White, and Edwin L. Godkin. The by-laws of 1887 provided that the meetings should be held in New York, Boston, or some intermediate point. The club was dominated by the believers in extreme laissez faire. They comprised the executive committee, which also served as the committee on membership. The executive committee decided the subject of discussion and, as the membership committee, proposed new members. Two black balls would defeat a prospective member. (A copy of the by-laws is attached to the letter from Laughlin to McCulloch, February 5, 1889, in the McCulloch Papers, University of Indiana Library.) The club had a fitful existence.

believed that such a statement would be issued by a substantial portion of the leadership of the profession.

As the nation moved on through the nineties, however,
the pace of reform slowed. As in the realm of affairs, so in
the realm of knowledge there are strong tides, and sometimes periods of reaction. The crest in the eighties gave
way to a period of stabilization and consolidation, a desire
for security, suspicion of innovations, and deprecation of
further reforms. There was almost no new reform legislation. The conservatism in Congress was paralleled in the
judiciary. The effectiveness of such important statutes as
the Interstate Commerce Commission Act and the Sherman Anti-Trust Act was for the time being curtailed by
decisions of the United States Supreme Court. Likewise,
the federal income tax was declared unconstitutional. In
1892 Congress drastically cut the appropriations for the
Geological Survey, reducing its functions to topography
alone, and Major Powell retreated to the safety of the
Bureau of American Ethnology. On the election of Mc-
Kinley to the presidency in 1896, Adams bemoaned what
he felt would be unchecked dominance by the business and
financial community: "We are destined to have during the
next four years a control of government by a class interest
and, to my mind, there is no hope." [45]
There was little enthusiasm for innovation in economic
analysis. For example, even the original leader in the
promotion of mathematical economics, Simon Newcomb,
voiced doubts of the usefulness of further work in this
field. He expressed the hope that economists would devote their energies to educating the public in the simpler
abstractions, as he called them, of the Ricardian economics
of an earlier age.
Economics had only just begun to have autonomy in an

---

[45] H. C. Adams to Albert Shaw, December 15, 1896, in Shaw Papers.

important area in its own right rather than as a limited narrow topic in moral philosophy. Particularly during such heated political struggles as "free silver," there was much feeling that moderation in matters of policy was essential to protect the infant profession. Moderation, however, took on the character of reaction when such a well-known figure in both learning and public affairs as Francis A. Walker could be accused by fellow economists of having brought the whole profession into disrepute by advocating such a mild measure as international bimetallism. Reinforcing the reaction was the use of the extreme individualistic view of evolution to support the gold standard. It was contended that this standard was "a natural evolution, not the creation of governments." [46]

Even the severe depression which began with a money panic in 1893 reinforced the belief among the overwhelming majority of respected monetary theorists that bimetallism or any deviation from the strict gold standard was out of the question. Nevertheless, as a contemporary maintained, one would have been hard put to find two experts who agreed on what should be the first step in solving the currency problem. So great was the divergence in views that the Chief of the Bureau of Statistics of the Treasury, after listening to the specialists for two fruitless hours, complained that "if the 'experts' talk thus, how can we expect the ordinary common sense man to comprehend the status of the question or much less to know of, or recognize, a remedy?" There was, of course, the implication that Horace White had stated so bluntly a decade before: that the common man could hardly respect the monetary expert.[47]

---

[46] *The Cabinet Diary of William L. Wilson, 1896–1897*, ed. by F. P. Summers (Chapel Hill: University of North Carolina Press, 1957), p. 130.

[47] W. C. Ford to Manton Marble, December 30, 1894, in Manton Marble Papers, Library of Congress. The letter contains an interesting account of

Statistical investigations might have been useful in help-
ing to solve some of the questions, but, instead of being
expanded, such work was hampered and even curtailed
because of inadequate funds and public indifference. One
of the best indications of the precarious status of statistical
inquiry was the absence of a permanent census organization prior to 1900.

During this period the marginal utility theory and its
correlate, marginal productivity, as developed by W. Stan-
ley Jevons, the Austrians, and J. B. Clark and synthesized
with the classical doctrines a few years later by Alfred
Marshall, came to the fore. Those who tended to narrow
the science seized upon marginalism as the key to a complete understanding of the workings of the economic system. Along this same line, they held that statistical and
historical research were of secondary importance. Utility
theory provided a unified model of an idealized, highly
automatic economic system. This in itself had great aesthetic appeal. A large segment of the profession, which
still held to a pleasure-pain psychology, found the mar-

what might be called a joint session in New York City of the Political
Economy Club and the American Economic Association:

"Last evening was held the Political Economy Club dinner, and it was by
far the most brilliant affair yet given. Horace White (the host) invited in
about 25 members of the Am. Economic Assn., so there was a surplus of
the 'academic' element. Mr. White opened with a paper on the currency,
a restatement of what he gave to Springer's [congressional] committee.
Professor Laughlin (fresh from his experiments on the black-beetles of
Hayti) followed, and gave a very flimsy criticism of [Secretary of the
Treasury] Carlisle's scheme (faulty enough, Heaven knows, without being
responsible for evils not contained in it). Mr. Hewitt said the public
would never consent to an abolition of the national bank system, and made
a plea for bank-issues with government inspection, and no government
issues. [Edward] Atkinson, as is his wont, made a good point by showing
that only 5% or less of transactions was settled in money (currency), and
if that 5% was protected, all would be well; but he ruined the point by
saying that personal local checks should be the ordinary money—as 95% of
transactions now are, etc. The prize fool was Thomas Shearman, who said
no money at all was needed—and thus the two hours ended in nothing."

ginal utility explanation of demand eminently satisfying. Moreover, to many vulgarizers utility theory represented an extension of natural law to the realm of economics. As a result, some issues which heretofore had been unsettled became dogmatically determined, especially that of the distribution of wealth.

Interestingly, the German-trained contingent had been the first to welcome Jevons' theory of marginal utility as a part of their new economics. They believed that it would throw considerable light on the determination of market price and would lead to fertile analyses of consumption, a field heretofore neglected by the orthodox. In much the same perspective, Adolf Wagner had written a highly sympathetic and influential review of Marshall's *Principles of Economics* in the *Quarterly Journal of Economics*. No more than Wagner, however, did the promoters of the new economics in the United States believe that economic science should be restricted to marginalism and the neoclassical system.

Many economists now directed their main attention to rather narrow, practical, and immediate ends, or so it seemed. Some of the older leaders of the movement for reconstruction went into administrative work; others specialized in less controversial subjects, such as public finance; still others devoted themselves to the rationale of the static state, but even these protected themselves against the charge of lack of immediate practical reference by claiming that their analyses tested the validity of the right of the existing economic system to survive. Social innovation was considered outside the realm of science.

The reaction that began in the late nineties begot in turn a counterreaction. The extreme rigidity and narrowness of dominant thinking seemingly provided an excellent target for the criticisms of Veblen and Commons.

It was at this point that institutionalism, as we know it now, reached maturity.

At about the same time, the Progressive movement got under way and soon reached its high point. I do not intend to imply that institutionalism in the social sciences and progressivism in politics are different sides of the same phenomenon. Of the three founders of institutionalism, only Commons had anything like a close connection with the Progressive movement, and even he did not support all features of its program. Both developments, however, were responses to the archconservatism that prevailed at the turn of the century.

In the new attempt to revitalize economics, the rebels had the support of some of the most orthodox economists of the seventies and eighties. For example, J. Laurence Laughlin in 1903 attempted, though with little success, to persuade the president of the St. Louis Congress of Arts and Science, Simon Newcomb, to expand the treatment of economics at the Congress to include:

a. Origin of Existing Economic Institutions
b. History of Economic Systems
c. Relation of Economics to 1) History, 2) Ethics, 3) Political Science, 4) Psychology [46]

Symptomatic, too, was the revived interest in the German historical school and in economic history. Renewed attention to the historical school was due largely to the appearance of the massive *Grundriss der allgemeinen Volkswirtschaftslehre* (*Outline of General Economic Theory*, 2 vols., 1900–1904) by Gustav Schmoller of Berlin, a

---

[46] Statement of Laughlin attached to letter from Laughlin to Simon Newcomb, March 27, 1903, in Newcomb Papers, Library of Congress. Laughlin complained to Newcomb that "in fact, among scientific men, there is possibly no full appreciation of the economics field." Laughlin to Newcomb, March 29, 1903, in Newcomb Papers.

treatise which insisted upon the connection between economics and other phenomena and the study of economic development. The University of California's A. C. Miller asserted in 1904 that Schmoller presented a "new type of economics, a type that attempts, and with appreciable success, to carry into the study of economic institutions something of the spirit and method of the later-day sciences." [49] The traditionalist Frank W. Taussig of Harvard, who for more than half a century exerted tremendous influence on American economic thinking, likewise praised Schmoller's work as "a remarkable survey of economics from the historical point of view; encyclopedic in its range, with admirable sketches of the great lines of industrial development and of present conditions, and broad-minded discussion of current social and economic problems." [50]

The revitalization of economic history was spearheaded by the recently established Carnegie Institution of Washington (1902). It appointed an advisory committee on economics, composed of Carroll D. Wright, as chairman, John Bates Clark, and Schmoller's student, Henry Farnam of Yale, to determine the most useful area for research that should be sponsored. It accepted the committee's recommendation for a monumental economic history of the United States. Wright, on behalf of the committee, expressed the feeling that the inquiry "should go beyond mere history, and should recognize the sociological results of economic development." [51] From this investigation came the broad-gauged works that firmly established John R. Commons as the nation's foremost authority on industrial

[49] Miller, "Economic Science in the Nineteenth Century," p. 44.

[50] F. W. Taussig, "Economic Theory," in *A Guide to Reading in Social Ethics and Allied Subjects*, ed. by Francis Peabody (Cambridge: Harvard University, 1910), p. 8.

[51] C. D. Wright, "An Economic History of the United States," *Publications of the American Economic Association*, 3d Series, Vol. VI, No. 2 (1905), p. 165.

relations—a position he still holds. Mitchell also obtained
recognition and a grant from the project to complete his
famous monetary study, *Gold, Prices, and Wages under
the Greenback Standard,* which was published by the
University of California Press.

The swelling volume of criticism of conventional theory
was reminiscent of the seventies and eighties. For example,
a prominent teacher with a good Harvard training, A. B.
Wolfe, complained that the age of scholastic orthodoxy
was again upon us. He explained the dilemma of the instructor:

> Suppose you are settled in your own mind as to the true the-
> ory of interest. . . . you give it to your class, and the next
> book a student takes up may give a theory so different from
> yours that he, dumbfounded, at once begins wondering
> whether economics is after all anything but philosophical
> hairsplitting. Or suppose that with academic catholicity you
> endeavor to initiate your sophomore into the mysteries of all
> the important theories of interest. It is then a question
> whether his knowledge of interest more resembles a well-
> scrambled egg, or a whirling dervish.[52]

At the same time there was further basic reconstruction
going on in related disciplines that reinforced the constructive enterprise of the founders of institutional theory.
Time is available for only a few examples. There was the
launching of sociological jurisprudence by Roscoe Pound,
then at the University of Nebraska, who was prodded on
by his sociologist-economist colleague and admirer of Veblen, E. A. Ross. While working on a Chicago newspaper,
Arthur F. Bentley, a trained economist, published the
greatest American contribution to political theory since
the *Federalist Papers.* This was *The Process of Government* (1908), which emphasized as the key the multiform

---

[52] A. B. Wolfe, "The Aim and Content of a College Course in Elementary
Economics," *Journal of Political Economy,* December 1909, p. 680.

group activities and interests as against a narrow range of class interests.

From the University of Michigan came a series of works by Charles Horton Cooley which stamped him as the most creative sociologist this country has produced. Were it not for the fact that only a small part of his work dealt directly with economic theory in general and institutional theory in particular, he might well have been considered a fourth founding father of institutional theory. He exercised a considerable influence on certain of his students who became leading institutionalists, such as Walton Hale Hamilton and Walter W. Stewart, and he has left a profound impress upon the nation's outstanding living economist, J. M. Clark. Clark has written that "Charles H. Cooley performed the great service of showing that the mechanism of the market, which dominates the values that purport to be economic, is not a mere mechanism for neutral recording of people's preferences, but a social institution with biases of its own, different from the biases of the institutions that purport to record, for example, aesthetic or ethical valuations. Policy-wise his theories looked largely in the direction of making the market responsive to a more representative selection of the values actually prevalent in the society." [53]

---

[53] J. M. Clark, "Aims of Economic Life as Seen by Economists," 1953, reprinted in his *Economic Institutions and Human Welfare* (New York: Knopf, 1957), p. 57. Clark held that what the exponents of institutional theory "had in common . . . was a refusal to accept the market as an adequate vehicle for expressing the importance of things to society. They looked beyond it in varying ways according to their differing personalities." *Ibid.*, p. 58.

Wesley C. Mitchell's description in 1914 of Veblen's "evolutionary" type of economic theory included his work on business cycles. "Veblen . . . gives us a brief study of the processes of cumulative change which have established the present system of business enterprise, a descriptive analysis of the ways in which these processes work at present, and a forecast of the probable course of cumulative changes which these processes and their contemporary cultural factors will probably follow in the future." Mitchell, Outline of lectures on "Types of Economic Theory," for April–May 1914.

There was, then, unquestionably a need for a treatment of economics going beyond the limited working scope of accepted theory. With their evolutionary view of economic activity as a component of, and only fully understandable in terms of, the cultural complex, the founders of institutionalism helped to meet this need. They recognized, to use the words of J. M. Clark, that "The problem of analysis starts at some existing point in our endless economic evolution, and is precipitated by some change from previously existing conditions." [54] Forming a background to their broad perspective of economics was their adherence to pragmatism in philosophy and to functionalism and behaviorism in psychology. Still, there was nothing approaching absolute uniformity in their ways of thinking. On the contrary, there were marked divergencies among all three. This was to be expected in view of the varied backgrounds and personalities, which led to substantial differences in the direction and in the emphasis of their work.

Veblen was the oldest and intellectually the most radical of the founders. He took for granted what he conceived to be sound in traditional value theory. His greatest contribution lay in the breadth and profusion of unusual insights that he produced by his anthropological approach to the culture of our times. Indeed, many of his ideas, although originally heatedly rejected, have over the years seeped into and become absorbed by our everyday mode of thinking. For example, his "pecuniary emulation" and "conspicuous consumption" have now become "the demonstration effect" in the analysis of demand and in the economics of underdeveloped countries. Similarly, "the instinct of workmanship" has found wide acceptance as a guiding principle, often under different labels. Furthermore, before Veblen wrote, dominant economic theory

---

[54] J. M. Clark, *Competition as a Dynamic Process*, p. 422.

hardly recognized the overwhelming importance of those two master institutions, the corporation and the machine technology. So commonplace have become a large number of the pregnant ideas and analyses that flowed so profusely from his fertile, disciplined mind, that today many of those who effectively use them are not aware of their source.[55] Perhaps Mitchell gave the key to an understanding of Veblen when in 1930 he described him as "the disturbing genius . . . that visitor from another world, who dissected the current commonplaces that the student had unconsciously acquired, as if the most familiar of his daily thoughts were curious products wrought in him by outside forces. No other such emancipator of the mind from the subtle tyranny of circumstance has been known in social science, and no other such enlarger of the realm of inquiry."[56]

As for Commons, his long career was marked by a wide range of investigations and interests devoted to making a place in economic theory for collective action in all its varieties, "a place which would be something more than a list of specific abuses or exceptions to laissez-faire. With this in view he broadened the concept of 'transaction' to include social action, and added the conceptions of a 'go-

---

[55] It is interesting to note that B. M. Anderson, Jr., who last taught at the University of California, pointed out some similarities between Joseph A. Schumpeter and Veblen, in his review of the original German edition of Schumpeter's most famous book, *The Theory of Economic Development* (*Political Science Quarterly*, December 1915). He wrote: "The psychology of Schumpeter's entrepreneur includes such elements as love of activity for its own sake, love of creative activity, love of distinction, love of victory over others, love of the game, and other traits which the newer psychology has been emphasizing, and with which such writings as those of Veblen . . . have made American students familiar. . . . The economist has too long been content with static theory, and work like that of Schumpeter and Veblen is full of significance for the better understanding of economic life."

[56] Mitchell, "Research in the Social Sciences," 1930, reprinted in his *The Backward Art of Spending Money and Other Essays*, ed. by Joseph Dorfman (New York: McGraw-Hill, 1937), p. 73.

ing concern' and its working rules—simultaneously broadened to include both private and social forms." [57] He
made two truly pioneering contributions: One was the
monumental historico-sociologico-oriented studies of such
major institutions as American trade unionism and Anglo-
American jurisprudence. The other was his active role as a
shaper of public policy. Again turning to Mitchell's apt
descriptions, he said in 1944 that Commons's "bent has
been toward inventing institutions, rather than [like Veb-
len] toward standing on the side lines and watching them
develop." [58]

Mitchell's own outstanding accomplishment was the establishment of quantitative analysis on a permanent basis.
Today public policy could not be effectively discussed or
administered without the vast, extensive statistical studies
regularly produced by various departments and agencies
of government and private research organizations. All
these investigations owe a debt to his pathbreaking *Business Cycles*. As Morris A. Copeland has pointed out,
"Mitchell's theory of business cycles [was] the first triumph of the empirical natural science method in the
study of the behavior of prices and production." [59]

Thus the differences among the members of the triumvirate added greatly to the richness, breadth, and far-
reaching and enduring influence of their work.

---

[57] J. M. Clark, "Aims of Economic Life as Seen by Economists," p. 58.

[58] Mitchell, "Outline of 12th Lecture of Seminar in Economic Change,
Columbia University, January 11, 1944," in Mitchell Papers, Columbia
University Libraries.

[59] M. A. Copeland, "Economic Theory and the Natural Science Point of
View," *American Economic Review*, March 1931, p. 77. Copeland's "Competing Products and Monopolistic Competition" (*Quarterly Journal of
Economics*, November 1940) is a good example of the effective use of
mathematical techniques by an institutionalist.

TWO

The Legacy of
Thorstein Veblen

Thorstein Veblen is commonly, and I think rightly, regarded as the founding father or guiding spirit of American institutionalism. But that circumstance seems not to make it any easier to define institutionalism or to identify the influence of Veblen. What is commonly said of Veblen—that his works are diffuse, vague, inchoate, and devoid of any sort of system—is also said of institutionalism. Veblen never laid claim to being the founder of a new "school" of economic thought, and in this, too, institutionalism has followed his example. Almost without exception those who have identified themselves as institutionalists have disavowed having any distinctive theory, economic or otherwise. What they have in common, and what they share with Veblen, has seemed even to themselves to be a compelling interest in the qualitative aspects of economic affairs, in what lies beyond the quantitative measurements of price—in the whole picture, so to speak.

Thus institutionalism has come to be regarded as supplementary to economics proper, a sort of fringe benefit. Virtually all the institutionalists—all that I can think of at the moment—have been academic men, members in more or less good repute of "regular" economics departments. They have been tolerated and even respected by their colleagues, much as sociologists are. Their good works, like those of sociologists, have been recognized and honored even when their explicitly economic character has been unclear.

What light does all this throw on the unique insights of Thorstein Veblen? We hold the principal author of the Federal Social Security Act in high esteem—but was his concern for the fate of the toiling masses derived from Veblen? And even if it was, how does that concern help us to identify Veblen's unique contribution to our thinking? That concern has been shared by many others in the main line of economic doctrine, notably by John Stuart Mill. Shall we try to identify Veblen's contribution in terms of what he held in common with John Stuart Mill?

I raise these questions only for purposes of direction. Surely it is clear that no superficial tabulation of common interests will serve our purpose. Veblen himself never said what he was driving at. The reason for this, I think, is not because he did not know. The point is rather that he was aiming so high that to have explicitly identified his target would have required a degree of self-aggrandizement that was entirely foreign to his character. For if he was right, that would have meant, as I shall try to show, that virtually all other economists were quite wrong—not just a little wrong in matters of detail such as can be readily corrected and even acknowledged without serious loss of face, but utterly and incorrigibly wrong. They were, he thought, proceeding in so wrong a direction that no amount of persistence in that direction would ever bring them right.

This, indeed, he did say. I do not see how anybody can read his critical essays—those, for example, which were reprinted in *The Place of Science in Modern Civilisation*

—with this question in mind and not reach this conclusion. Veblen is not trying here to set marginal utility theory, for example, on the right track. He is saying the track itself is utterly wrong. But he did not point clearly to what he regarded as the right track. To have done so would have required Olympian egotism. Such Olympians exist. But Veblen was not one of them.

What Veblen was trying to suggest, from his earliest writings to his latest, was not only a different economics, but a different conception of the economy itself.

Economics is the study of the economy, and its most basic concept is therefore that of the economy itself. In this respect economics runs true to scientific form. Chemistry, for example, is usually defined as the study of substances; and it then develops that chemistry employs a very special conception of what a substance is. This conception turns upon the distinction—one that is therefore basic to the whole science—between elements and compounds. Indeed, as everybody knows, modern chemistry was founded upon this distinction; that is, upon the discovery that some substances cannot be reduced to anything else, whereas others can be shown to be combinations of various of those irreducible substances. The subject matter of economics, likewise, has often been described with truly sublime vagueness, for example as "the ordinary business of living." But economists also have a very special conception of what they mean by ordinary business, and in their case, too, the whole discipline is founded upon that conception. This is based on the discovery that the various activities in which people engage in getting a living are knit together in a sort of system. It is this system that has come to be known as the economy, and so is the subject matter of economics. Thus, the master question of economics is, What is the nature of this system?

It is true of economics, as it is of chemistry, that a great deal of work more or less contributory to later understanding was done before any decisive answer was given to this question. But at this point the analogy breaks down. For in the case of chemistry the concept of elemental substances is so clear and decisive that it makes a clean break with all previous theorizing. In economics just the opposite has been the case. That is, curious observers of the system became deeply committed to particular conceptions of it long before they became aware that what they were observing constitutes a system.

The reasons for this are many and curious. For example, quite early in modern times—two or three centuries before the phrase "political economy" began to be used—statesmen and their advisers became increasingly aware of various automatic adjustments in which the whole community participated in such a way as to bring about results which were no part of their intention. Thus, indirect taxes blend with the prices of the affected goods and are not recognized. Coin clipping results in the disappearance of unclipped coins and a compensatory rise in price levels. In such considerations the attention of curious minds focused on the market as, seemingly, the guiding mechanism of the economy, an entity which was not yet conceived as such.

At the same time, merchants were becoming increasingly conspicuous. The activities of husbandmen and craftsmen are in the highest degree undramatic. Such people are drudges. The community takes them and their occupations for granted. But mystery and high drama suffuse the activities of merchants. From medieval times, the fair was an exciting break in the humdrum of existence. It was important. Merchants were increasingly important people. Buying and selling seemed to be the master key to a community's material existence.

Not for nothing is the whole body of economic literature

from the dawn of modern times to the middle of the eighteenth century known as mercantilism. The writers of this period had no common set of principles and no common program. Indeed, it has been said that the only thing they had in common was self-interest. What this means is that although thinkers of this period had not yet grasped the idea of the economy as a system of related activities they were unanimous in their obsession with mercantile activities.

Thus, when the concept of an economy did emerge, it was conceived by minds already long focused upon the activities of merchants, upon buying and selling, upon exchange, upon the market as the guiding mechanism of the economy. The "simple and obvious system" was not flashed suddenly upon the world by the genius of Adam Smith. Hints of it are to be found in the seventeenth century, for instance in the works of Petty and Boisguilbert. By the middle of the eighteenth century it was endemic. Jevons's excitement over his exhumation of Cantillon was due precisely to the fact that Cantillon's *Essai* anticipated by three years Quesnay's celebrated *Tableau oeconomique,* with its cardio-vascular theory of the circulation of wealth.

This is the conception of the economy against which Veblen rebelled. What has kept it alive and even enlisted some of the best minds of succeeding generations in its elaboration is its unique plausibility. Dissident writers have denounced it all along as an apology for what Marx taught us to call capitalism, and so it is. But it remains convincing, for it appeals to the common sense (as Veblen called it) of the community. Markets exist. They are everywhere. We all seem to live by buying and selling. The creation of wealth by the sweat of the brow—by guiding a plow or swinging a scythe, or even by driving the tractor that hauls a combine—continues to appear to most men to be a dull, unexciting, and insignificant business. What is significant, one feels, is the price one gets for his year's work. It is in the sale of the product that the ordinary business of living seems to reach its climax. Hence a buying-and-selling theory of how we live continues to seem, as it has seemed throughout modern times, supremely applicable.

Why, then, did Veblen reject it? Three answers to this question are commonly advanced. One is that he succumbed to subversive influences. Another is that he was a country boy who never felt quite at home in the hurly-burly of the modern market place. The third is that he was a misfit who could never hold a job, never made any money, and was bitterly envious of those who did. There may be an element of truth in such pronouncements. Veblen did read Edward Bellamy's *Looking Backward,* and Dorfman quotes Veblen's wife as saying, "I believe that this was the turning point in our lives." [1] He was a country boy who hated typewriters and telephones; he seems never to have driven a car or to have had a brokerage account. Certainly he never achieved wealth.

But, whatever the effects of these experiences, what seems to me much more significant is that he was enabled, by a different set of circumstances, to view the economy in a totally different perspective. Veblen seems to have viewed modern Western economy in the perspective of primitive society. From his student days onward, primitive culture was one of Veblen's most intense and continuous interests. I do not mean to suggest that this interest alone was responsible for shaping his conception of the nature of the economy. Many influences are at work in the life of every man, and in Veblen's case one has only to read Dorfman to realize how many and varied were those to which his subject

---

[1] Joseph Dorfman, *Thorstein Veblen and His America* (New York: Viking Press, 1934) , p. 68.

was exposed. Nevertheless, the correspondence between the anthropological conception of the economy and that of Veblen is too close to be ignored.

According to the anthropologists, every culture includes an economy. In a sense this observation merely states a truism, that every community has some way of getting a living. The significant refinement of this observation is that each society has its own distinctive way of getting a living. Among simple peoples, some single food source is usually so important a feature of getting a living that their economies can be meaningfully identified with their respective foods. Thus we recognize fish cultures, taro cultures, yak cultures, and so on. There is some evidence that the earliest known human inhabitants of Europe had a mammoth culture.

At first blush it appears that the economies of advanced civilizations, and especially that of the modern Western world, do not lend themselves to similar designation. For the more advanced a people is, the more varied is its dietary. But a moment's reflection will resolve this difficulty, and the resolution will be borne out by the facts. The truth is that every economy, however simple, is technologically based. In order for a particular article of food to have become the mainstay of any people, that people must have developed suitable tools and techniques for obtaining that food substance. The mammoth hunters who followed the retreating continental glacier, living off the huge pachyderms which fed on the vegetation of the tundra, are known to have specialized in calves. They must have developed specialized techniques for cutting the calves out of the herds and then dispatching them. They may even have used glacial ice as a ready-made deep freeze. Indeed, all food-designated economies are in fact specialized tool-and-technique economies. Thus, whole cultures have been transformed by the introduction of new

instruments. When the plains Indians of the Old West obtained horses from the Spaniards, they abandoned their
ancient corn technology and began following the herds of
bison. As identified by their principal source of food, theirs
was now a bison economy. But its real foundation was
horses and horsemanship.

To Veblen, therefore, industrial technology is the real
substance of the modern economy. This conception of the
economy is not a denial of the existence of its market
aspect. But which is the dog and which is the tail? No ex-
ponent of the market theory has ever denied the existence
of what Veblen called "the machine process." That theory,
however, implies that the creative principle somehow in-
heres in the market, or in the price system, or in the profit
motive, or even in competition. Some exponents of this
conception of the economy have even gone so far as to attribute all the features of modern civilization—not only
machine technology but even science itself, and not only
science but all the arts, indeed all the achievements of the
human spirit—to the market mentality. Absurd as such
claims are, they are only an exaggeration of the concept
that has been basic to our economic thinking throughout
modern times. As Adam Smith put it, "As it is the power
of exchanging that gives occasion to the division of labour,
so the extent of this division must always be limited by the
extent of that power, or, in other words, by the extent of
the market." [2]

Veblen's conception of the economy is the exact reverse
of this, and can be most succinctly stated in these very
words. As it is the state of the industrial arts that gives
occasion to exchange, so the extent of the market must always be limited by the state of the industrial arts. This con-

---

[2] Adam Smith, *The Wealth of Nations,* edited by Edwin Cannan (5th
ed.; London: Methuen & Co., 1930) , Vol. I, p. 19.

ception of the economy, which it is the business of economics to seek to understand, is Veblen's principal legacy.

It is quite true that a clear and explicit statement to this effect cannot be found in any of Veblen's published works. But what can be found—what has been found by all serious students of his work—is an obsessive preoccupation with the interplay of two conflicting forces. His first book, *The Theory of the Leisure Class,* opens with the following sentences:

> The institution of a leisure class is found in its best development at the higher stages of the barbarian culture; as, for instance, in feudal Europe or feudal Japan. In such communities the distinction between classes is very rigorously observed; and the feature of the most striking economic significance in these class differences is the distinction maintained between the employments proper to the several classes. The upper classes are by custom exempt or excluded from industrial occupations, and are reserved for certain employments to which a degree of honour attaches [and with a characteristic touch of irony, Veblen spells "honor" with a "u"]. Chief among the honourable employments in any feudal company is warfare; and priestly service is commonly second to warfare. . . . Under this ancient distinction the worthy employments are those which may be classed as exploit; unworthy are those necessary everyday employments into which no appreciable element of exploit enters.[3]

Note especially Veblen's use here of the phrase "industrial occupations." In the following year he wrote his celebrated essay on "Industrial and Pecuniary Employments," and four years later this distinction—in essence, between making things and making money—became the subject of his second book, *The Theory of Business Enterprise.*

[3] *The Theory of the Leisure Class* (New York: Macmillan, 1899), pp. 1, 8.

A little farther along in *The Theory of the Leisure Class*, we come upon another of his basic distinctions, a reference ". . . to another force, alien, and in some degree antagonistic, to the usage of conspicuous waste. This alien factor is the instinct of workmanship." [4] A year earlier the *American Journal of Sociology* had published Veblen's article on "The Instinct of Workmanship and the Irksomeness of Labor," and fourteen years later his third book bore the title, *The Instinct of Workmanship*.

In his essay entitled "Why Is Economics Not an Evolutionary Science?" published a year before *The Theory of the Leisure Class*, Veblen raised a question which has been thrown up to institutionalists as a challenge ever since: If the law of supply and demand, the theory of price equilibrium, marginal analysis, and all that, are to be cast aside, what has institutionalism to put in its place? Veblen phrased the question as follows: "If we are getting restless under the taxonomy of a monocotyledonous wage doctrine and a cryptogamic theory of interest, with involute, loculicidal, tomentous and moniliform variants, what is the cytoplasm, centrosome, or karyokinetic process to which we must turn, and in which we may find surcease from the metaphysics of normality and controlling principles? What are we going to do about it?" [5] I think it would be fair to say that the professional consensus is that neither Veblen nor any of his institutionalist followers has done anything about it. In a sense this charge is true. That is, neither Veblen nor any institutionalist has devised any theory of how the market-guided economy works. None has done so for a very simple reason—as Veblen and the institutionalists see it, that is not the problem. "What have

---

[4] *Ibid.*, p. 93.

[5] *Quarterly Journal of Economics*, July 1898, reprinted in *The Place of Science in Modern Civilisation* (New York: Huebsch, 1919), 1932 ed. (Viking), p. 70.

you to put in its place?" typically assumes the validity of the traditional conception of the economy and in effect challenges institutionalists to present a nonpecuniary price theory, a nonmarket portrayal of the market.

But rejection of the traditional conception of the economy is the starting point of Veblen's economics and, I think, the keynote of institutionalism generally. Veblen's commitment to a differently conceived economy seems to me quite clear. For in the essay from which I have just quoted his famous botanical ironies—and mind you, this essay was published in 1898!—he goes right on to say that the issue is not what are we going to do but what are we now doing: "There is the economic life process still in great measure awaiting theoretical formulation. The active material in which the economic process goes on is the human material of the industrial community. For the purpose of economic science the process of cumulative change that is to be accounted for is the sequence of change in the methods of doing things—the methods of dealing with the material means of life." [6] In short, from his earliest systematic writings to his last, Veblen was preoccupied with "workmanship" and "exploit" because he was convinced that only in such terms could the economic life process—the ordinary business of living—be understood.

History is already hard at work proving Veblen right. These categories, which are so wildly irrelevant to the apparatus of price equilibrium, are now generally recognized as the master principles of economic development. To be sure, they are not commonly discussed in Veblenese, and I do not mean to claim that the concurrence of present-day thinking with Veblenian principles is directly traceable to Veblen's influence. But the significance of any man's work

---

[6] *Ibid.*, pp. 70–71.

—the value of his legacy—depends on what happens afterward. The voyages of Columbus were important precisely because, although he never dreamed of it, two vast continents lay west of the Atlantic. He was part of a tremendous movement, and so, in a somewhat different sense, was Veblen.

To appreciate the significance of Veblen's principles we must be prepared to take several liberties with his categories. He identified "workmanship" and "exploit" as instincts, and even identified these instincts with hereditary racial characteristics. But present-day science has turned its face away from instincts and racial types. Hence it is easy to dismiss Veblen's whole analytical methodology as nonsense, especially since his conception of instincts and of racial types is so extraordinarily vague. Furthermore, not content with inventing two instincts, Veblen surrounded each with a cluster of related propensities. Thus workmanship is somehow manifest in the "parental bent" and even in "idle curiosity"—or is it the other way around? And the same is true of exploit. It is somehow related to, or manifest in, ostentation, snobbery, ritualism, and archaism. Thus the impulses which lead to warfare are akin to the horror with which academicians react to "tropartic" motor oil and cigarettes that taste "like a cigarette should." As the Master said in the penultimate paragraph of *The Theory of the Leisure Class:*

A discriminate avoidance of neologisms is honorific . . . As felicitous an instance of futile classicism as can well be found, outside the Far East, is the conventional spelling of the English language. A breach of the proprieties in spelling is extremely annoying and will discredit any writer in the eyes of all persons who are possessed of a developed sense of the true and beautiful. English orthography satisfies all the requirements of the canons of reputability under the law of conspicuous waste. It is archaic, cumbrous and ineffective; its acquisition consumes much time and effort; failure to acquire it is easy of detection. Therefore it is the first and readiest test of reputability in learning, and conformity to its ritual is indispensable to a blameless scholastic life.

Is this just amusing nonsense? If not, what was Veblen driving at?

For one thing, he saw that there are certain forms or types of behavior which are extraordinarily persistent throughout life and throughout history. When he began to play with these ideas, the notion of instinct was in good odor, and he therefore adopted it—but not without misgivings. Just how this mechanism worked neither Veblen nor anybody else was very sure, and Veblen was therefore pretty vague about it—as he might have said, scrupulously vague. But he was quite clear and definite about the persistence, and in this, later work has borne him out.

For another thing, Veblen saw, as pagan philosophers and Christian theologians had seen, how important is the polarity of human life. Thus, although he never says so, just as he never presents us with a definitive list of instincts, his instincts form two clusters, one creative and the other obstructive, one dynamic and the other inhibitory. Just why this is so Veblen also never says. But he does say how, and the how implies the why. Workmanship implies working not only with the hands but with tools, and tools are always capable of combination and elaboration. Growth, development, evolution—all are implicit in that type of activity. On the other hand, honor, prestige, and propriety necessarily look to the past. At every point their criterion is authenticity, and authenticity means of and from the past. That is why "considerations of use and wont," or, to employ another favorite Veblenian phrase, "imbecile institutions," are a drag on the evolutionary process that springs from technology: they are inherently past-binding.

On both sides of this dichotomy Veblen has been borne out by twentieth-century developments. His attribution of the technical progress of mankind to the inherent dynamism of "workmanship" coincides with all that we have been able to learn of the history of science and the process of invention. What are discovery and invention but the serendipity of the laboratory and the machine shop? And what is serendipity but idle curiosity, the free play of the inquiring mind? The secret of progress is research: such is the motto of the twentieth century.

Or is it that we must break the bonds of the past? On this side, also, the modern mind agrees with Veblen. As Western society becomes ever more fluid, contemporary scholarship becomes increasingly aware of persistence and pervasiveness of class, status, hierarchy. The very phrase "status symbol," which might have come straight from the pages of Veblen (but did not) , has become a cliché of mid-twentieth-century conversation. The British system of monetary values—pounds, shillings, and pence—which vies with English orthography as an instance of futile classicism, is at last going down before the stern necessities of electronic computers; and—who knows?—when the computers learn to correspond with each other they may at long last rationalize the English language.

Veblen is also receiving confirmation from the development of under-industrialized regions where "the process of cumulative change" is most dramatic. For one thing, the drama of economic development is bringing home to us the significance of the technological process. "Foreign aid" clearly demonstrates what Veblen called "the merit of borrowing." The Cubans are not beginning where the Wright Brothers began; they are getting MIGs from the Soviet Union and sending their boys to Czechoslovakia for pilot training. Meanwhile, industrial revolution is thwarted by the persistence of "use and wont." Sacred cows continue to wander through the fields and villages of India. Never has the Veblenian polarity of industrial technology and imbecile institutions been more clearly manifest than in the population explosion, which, as Luis Muñoz Marin once said, is a product of the coexistence of "an industrial death rate and a pre-industrial birth rate."

There is still another respect in which history may be said to be on Veblen's side. Far more than it was even in Veblen's day, economics is now an empirical science. The classical doctrine of the automatically self-regulating market contra-indicates not only regulation but even observation. Since regulation is unnecessary and unwise, detailed scrutiny of the economy also is unnecessary. The earlier classical economists were therefore extraordinarily incurious as to what was actually going on. Indeed, this was a major issue in the *Methodenstreit* between the devotees of automaticity and the historical school. By the time of Veblen's formative years, various circumstances—the railways, the trusts, the labor movement—had begun to command the attention of even the most cloistered scholars. This, I think, is what Veblen meant by his reference, in 1898, to "what we are now doing."

Even so, our present students, schooled as they are in macro-economics, must find it hard to realize that as recently as the time when some of us were pursuing our Ph.D.'s there was no statistical gauge of the performance of the economy. It was not until several years after the end of the First World War that the Federal Reserve index of industrial production was defined and that invaluable statistical series was established; and the GNP, which today everybody rattles off as though it came over on the *Mayflower*, is even more recent.

A little recent history is of interest in this regard. The National Bureau of Economic Research was set up in

1920. From the first, the Bureau was primarily interested in national income accounting. The pioneer work of several distinguished scholars sponsored by the Bureau was the basis on which, beginning in the middle thirties, the Department of Commerce undertook to measure the Gross National Product, with the result that the most important statistical series in the world—the GNP of the USA—was established just before Pearl Harbor.

To attribute this whole development to the influence of Thorstein Veblen would be easily refuted exaggeration. Empirical studies of one kind or another now absorb a considerable part of the time and energies of nearly all economists, most of whom have small knowledge of and less interest in Veblen. Doubtless something very like what has happened would have occurred if Veblen had never lived. The importance of these developments for an understanding of the legacy of Thorstein Veblen lies not in any direct causal sequence, but in the degree to which they validate his conception of the economic life process. The whole national income approach to the study of the economy is in a quite literal sense Veblenian, although he never used the term "macro-economics" or uttered the magic initials "GNP."

It is, however, an interesting fact that both the creator of the Federal Reserve index of industrial production and the founder of the National Bureau were directly influenced by Veblen. The former, Walter W. Stewart, had been a student and junior colleague of Veblen's at the University of Missouri; the latter, Wesley Mitchell, had been a graduate student at the University of Chicago during the years when Veblen was writing *The Theory of Business Enterprise*. Whatever the genius of Mitchell or Stewart, no one ever starts from scratch. Veblen loved to point to "larger forces moving obscurely in the background," and the phrase might well be applied to him. He himself was a larger force moving obscurely in the background.

In a very basic sense, then, what we now call macro-economics is Veblenian economics, notwithstanding the fact that Keynes did more than anyone else to establish macro-economics as a distinct discipline. The central concept is Veblenian. As I have tried to show, what dominated Veblen's thinking from his earliest economic essays to his latest was a conception of the economy quite different from that to which the great writers of the classical tradition had somehow become committed. He conceived the economy as the system of related activities by which the people of any community get their living. This system embraces a body of knowledge and of skills and a stock of physical equipment; it also embraces a complex network of personal relations reinforced by custom, ritual, sentiment, and dogma. This conception of the economy—one that is applicable to a paleolithic culture no less than to our own, and to our own no less than to any other—is Thorstein Veblen's principal bequest to succeeding generations.

Macro-economics is Veblenian precisely in the sense that it turns away from the sterilities of price equilibrium theory to the realities of the community's efforts to feed and clothe and house itself. This is what Keynes prevailed upon us to do, pointing out that in such an affluent society as ours people go hungry not because of any inexorable laws but only because we choose to do as we do in respects that are quite amenable to alteration. And Keynes, of course, was not the only one. Many of us remember the excitement with which we read the Brookings Institution studies of *America's Capacity to Produce* and *America's*

Capacity to Consume. Now, we felt, economics is getting down to business—the business of finding out how we are doing in the ordinary business of living.

But, I have often been told with a touch of exasperation, all these studies employ price data. Yes, of course they do. In so complex an economy as ours, they must. But that is not the point. It was price theory, not price data, against which Veblen declaimed: the theory that prices serve as a guiding hand to lead mankind to maximize utility. I will not deny that Veblen sometimes exaggerated, or that his followers—including, I regret to say, myself—have sometimes talked as though all prices were somehow suspect. But fortunately this matters very little. It matters very little whether Veblen is correctly understood or not. Indeed, he would have been the last to assert a claim to absentee ownership of blameless scholastic reputation.

What does matter is our conception of our task. To get significant answers one must ask significant questions. More and more, I think, we are learning to ask significant questions. Why does the economy of the United States, the richest in the world, grow at a rate less than half that of the recently devastated countries of Europe? Why does unemployment persist, and even increase, in periods of growing prosperity? In my view, questions such as these reveal the significance of Veblen's legacy. But whether that is recognized or not, whether it is true or not, is a relatively unimportant matter of scholastic history. What is most important is getting the best answers we can to the best questions we can ask today.

THREE

The Institutional Economics
of John R. Commons

John R. Commons was a son of the Middle Border. The roots of his institutional economics were planted in the disorderly economic development of his beloved Middle West of the first quarter of this century, and in many ways his economic thinking shared the disorderliness of his own institutional involvements. He assimilated raw experiences as some statisticians assimilate raw data, and, just as the statistician sometimes finds problems in classifying data to arrive at homogeneous categories and meaningful generalizations, so Commons encountered difficulties in sorting out his experiences and impressions and molding them into useful economic concepts. In a homespun and often disingenuous way, he strove with dogged persistence to combine active personal participation in the economic fray with an intellectual search for the broader meaning of the particular instance. His pattern was to move from cases to concepts. In the social sciences, the process of conceptualization enjoys at best a transient success, and it is problematical how much of a direct impact Commons succeeded in making on the mainstream of economic thinking. But his indirect influence on the thinking of innumerable students and colleagues was unquestionably telling.

There was nothing smooth or commonplace about the academic career of John R. Commons, and a few biographical details add not only interest in the man but understanding of his work. He spent his boyhood in Ohio and Indiana, the son of a father remarkable more for a dilettante intellectual curiosity than for business acumen. A backslider from Quakerism, the senior Commons apparently moved through stages of agnosticism and spiritualism and then Christian Science. He tried unsuccessfully to establish a hometown newspaper and seems to have wound up depending for survival on the efforts of his more disciplined wife. John's mother, with fortitude supplied at least in part by a rigorous Presbyterianism, was the principal provider. When the decision was made that John was to go to Oberlin, it was in large part his mother who made this financially possible by moving to Oberlin with him and there running a boarding house. John and his brother found work as part-time printers in Cleveland, some 30 miles away, and there John began absorbing some of the raw experiences of the workplace out of which he was later to fashion his concepts of collective action.

His record at Oberlin hardly stamped him as having superior intellectual powers. He candidly admits that he graduated at 26 "by the indulgence of my professors." Indeed, much of his academic career is singularly devoid of the usual marks of success. For a number of years he seemed to move on from one failure to another. Perhaps the secret lay in just that—he kept moving, piling up the rich store of raw experiences on which he was later to draw.

From Oberlin he went, on borrowed funds and through the good offices of one of his professors, to Johns Hopkins, where Richard T. Ely was indoctrinating a clutch of earnest young graduate students in his "go and see" method of social inquiry. John threw himself with great enthusiasm into his field assignments, among other things a stint as case worker for the Charity Organization Society. The immediate problems of the charity cases of Baltimore were of little help in mastering the content of economic history, however, and a failure in examinations in that field washed away all hope of the fellowship on which he was relying to complete his graduate degree. He was more than grateful, he was also a little surprised, when his Hopkins professors were willing to recommend him for an instructorship at Wesleyan University. He never did complete his doctorate.

Wesleyan added one more item to the unspectacular career which Commons was carving out for himself. Three months before the end of the academic year, the President called him in to break the news that his services would not be needed the following year. The young instructor was given to understand that his teaching had been something less than distinguished, and that his students had shown a remarkable lack of interest.

The experience was a bitter one, especially since he was now married and with a child on the way, but he later wrote in his autobiography that he had profited from it. A prospective teacher might be interested in his diagnosis, although I do not report it with unqualified endorsement. He concluded that he had failed as a teacher because he had tried to be too systematic in his approach to the subject of economics, retailing abstractions without providing adequate feel for the underlying realities from which the abstractions were derived. Empty formalism was the consequence. "I determined," he wrote,

. . . that I would spring on my next students all of my inconsistencies, all of my doubts of economic theory, all of my little schemes for curing economic, political, and sociological disease. Perhaps that would interest them. . . . Henceforth, for more than forty years, they could see that I was not an authority, did not know much of anything, but was getting ideas from them, and incorporating their ideas into mine. . . . Every class meeting or lecture was something unexpected, and they didn't know what was coming next. I was continually changing my mind.[1]

There followed a brief sojourn at his alma mater, Oberlin, before he was given an appointment at the University of Indiana, in his boyhood state. He appears to have enjoyed his stay there, and his departure was not entirely volitional. As he himself says, he made "another mistake." By somewhat unorthodox channels his name was proposed to Syracuse University as someone that institution should consider for a new chair in sociology. The chancellor wrote to him inquiring whether he would be interested. In a ploy which has become familiar to countless thousands of academic people over the years, Commons went to the Indiana administration to report the "offer" which he had received, in hopes of parlaying a salary increase but with no intent to leave. To his chagrin he was advised to accept the Syracuse appointment, which he did with reluctance. But he had learned another lesson, which may contain a useful grain of advice for those who are making their way up the academic ladder, particularly in these days when so many colleges and universities are tempting them to restlessness with offers of fast promotions and magnificent salary increases. "Never since," he said, "have I asked for an increase of salary. The exposure is too dangerous. But I have always asked for short hours and provision for a secretary and an assistant." [2]

Commons's stay at Syracuse was also of short duration.

---

[1] *Myself* (New York: Macmillan, 1934) , p. 47.
[2] *Ibid.*, p. 52.

His penchant for making trouble for himself continued to operate in high gear. He left Syracuse under something of a cloud for having advocated recreational facilities for amateur sports for Sunday use, the only day that working-men could enjoy them, at the same time that he opposed professional Sunday baseball. He thus managed to offend both religious and commercial sensibilities of the local interests. On his departure he was warned that probably no university in the country would be willing to hire him.

There then followed a series of temporary assignments, including the preparation of a report on immigration for the Industrial Commission which had been appointed by President McKinley and field work for the National Civic Federation. In 1904 Professor Ely called him to the University of Wisconsin, to which Ely had moved from Hopkins. Commons writes with feeling: "I was born again when I entered Wisconsin, after five years of incubation." [3]

The very next year he became involved in state affairs when he was asked by Governor LaFollette to help draft civil service legislation. We tend to think of Commons as being a labor economist, but both in his public and teaching roles he ventured into an amazing variety of fields. He taught and wrote on public utility regulation, monetary control, pricing practices, industrial organization, and taxation. His contributions on the legislative or action front involved civil service reform, factory legislation, workmen's compensation, unemployment insurance, small-loan interest-rate control, rural credit and taxation measures, inheritance taxation, property assessment laws, immigration laws, and monetary policy in addition to the industrial relations for which he is best known.

Personal tragedy dogged the later years of his life. World War I involved him in a deeply emotional way. A

---

[3] *Ibid.*, p. 95.

son in the expeditionary force was injured and later disappeared from home. His wife, his close companion and editorial reliance, died in 1928. His financial condition was precarious. He suffered from periodic breakdowns in health. On retirement he went to live with a sister in a Florida trailer camp. A postscript to his autobiography of 1934 reads simply: "My sister Anna was killed in an auto accident while this book was in press." His principal consolation was the loyalty displayed by numbers of his former students.

Despite these afflictions of mind and body, *Institutional Economics,* perhaps his major work, and *The Economics of Collective Action,* a synthesis of his work, were published in these less happy years. He died while visiting a sister in North Carolina in 1945.

BACKGROUND OF COMMONS'S INSTITUTIONALISM

The extensive writings of Professor Commons up to 1924 showed relatively little interest in economic theory. There was, it is true, a penetrating analysis of the impact on union organization and collective bargaining of the extension of product markets, which appeared in the *Quarterly Journal of Economics* in 1910, and which constitutes in my judgment the finest single exhibit in his lengthy bibliography, if not the finest single piece of research in the literature of labor economics. Drawing on a detailed historical knowledge of the development of the shoe industry in the United States, he derived historical generalizations which foreshadowed his later interests. But on the whole his attention and writing were absorbed in specific reform programs and particular institutions. What was not then apparent was that all the specific experience and direct observation, the personal involvement and the case study, were simply ingredients which, over the years, would be molded and shaped in the reflective processes of the mind into concepts of general applicability, designed to reduce the welter of casual and transient experience into a more orderly and comprehensible pattern.

In 1924 appeared the first of his two major theoretical works, *The Legal Foundations of Capitalism.* In the opening sentence of the preface he states his objective—the construction of a theory of value. The first, tentative gropings towards this objective, he said, had begun

thirty-five years ago at Johns Hopkins under my stimulating teacher, Richard T. Ely. . . . Afterwards I had various opportunities for the investigation of labor problems and problems connected with the regulation and valuation of public utilities. This led to a testing of economic and legal theories in the drafting of bills as an assistant to legislative committees in Wisconsin.

It was this experience, shared by my students, that led directly to the theoretical problems of this book. We had to study the decisions of the courts, if the new laws were to be made constitutional, and that study ran into the central question, What do the courts mean by reasonable value?

. . . I went to work with my students digging directly out of the court decisions stretching over several hundred years the behavioristic theory of value on which they were working. We were puzzled, for we tried to reconcile the economists from Quesnay to Cassel with the lawyers from Coke to Taft. We found eventually that what we were really working upon was not merely a theory of Reasonable Value but the Legal Foundations of Capitalism itself.

This large-scale project was undertaken, as he notes, with one eye on the relevant concepts of the economists of the period since the physiocrats. In the next ten years he reversed the process, concentrating on the value concepts of the economists in an historical and evolutionary sweep be-

ginning with John Locke, with one eye on the courts and
legal writers. For Commons, however, law and economics
were never sharply separated. Law (in the very broad
sense of the working rules of a society, going back to the
notion of sovereignty and the kinds and degrees of liberties
and immunities enjoyed under it) was an essential, indeed, the most essential ingredient forming the economic
relationships of a people.

COLLECTIVE ACTION

The first great simplifying concept which Commons offers
is *collective action,* which he makes almost synonymous
with institutionalism. But to understand what he means by
collective action requires some elaboration.

Society is characterized by a necessary conflict of interest among its constituent members, a conflict of interest
arising out of property rights in scarce resources. In some
imagined primitive societies there may have been such an
abundance of natural elements that men could satisfy their
needs without conflict, since there was enough for all, but
once nature is recognized as niggardly rather than benef-
icent, as requiring some orderly means of allocating limited wealth among many claimants, property rights enter
and conflict of interest emerges. A man does not "own" his
product because he has merged his labor with freely
available resources, as Locke had maintained. Resources
are not free but are scarce and subject to private title, and
the laborer is not entitled to the fruits of his own labor if
those fruits first require access to other's assets. Exchanges
of goods and services must take place, on terms reflecting
the relative propertied advantages and disadvantages of
the negotiators.

But society restricts property rights just as it bestows

them. It limits claims no less than it confirms them. The rights of property ownership are hedged about by a variety of restrictions on their exercise at the same time that the owner is given certain protections in their enjoyment and immunities from their infringement. "The term 'property' cannot be defined except by defining all the activities which individuals and the community are at liberty or required to do or not to do, with reference to the object claimed as property." [4] It is the fabric of social relationships which grow up in a community or a society which molds the nature of property, affecting its scarcity value. And these relationships change over time.

The basic property right is the legal power to withhold something from the use of others. That something need not be tangible or corporeal. As long as it represents a source of income which is legally unavailable to others, it constitutes a property right. A firm's goodwill is an obvious example, or a utility's franchise giving it future rights of operation which exclude others. The notion of intangible property rights embraces all sanctioned and protected expectations of future income flows.

When Commons speaks of collective action, then, he is not referring simply to the activities of organizations such as business firms and labor unions, trade associations and governmental agencies. These are of course included—"going concerns," he calls them, organized groups performing specific functions, containing conflicts of interests within themselves (among their members) and also opposing the conflicting interests of other such going concerns. But in addition to collective action of this organized variety Commons includes unorganized custom, the laws of the state and the common law of the courts, the total bundle of patterns of conduct which a society sanctions or com-

---

[4] *Institutional Economics* (New York: Macmillan, 1934) , p. 74.

pels of its members. Even when an individual engages in
a simple exchange with another individual, he acts within a
framework of collective law and custom, so that collective
action has in fact structured the relationship.

Social custom and law are in fact the product of these
interactions. People are not simply adapters to a code of
property law, or conformers to a body of customs affecting
the scarcity value of property ownership. In the process of
dealing with each other, bargaining, negotiating, transact-
ing, compromising, they bend and mold the customs,
modify the judicial gloss on the law, help to create the
very customs which affect their economic relationships.
Collective action thus controls the individual; but the individual has some power (especially in concerted effort
with others) to modify the nature of collective control.

But collective action is more than control of individual
action. By controlling the actions of some, it makes possible the actions of others; it frees them from coercion and
forms of competition which have been branded as "unfair." By controlling the actions of some, as through the
working rules of organizations, it enormously expands
the capabilities of those who manage such organizations
beyond the powers which they would have been able otherwise to wield on their own.

It is thus that Commons comes to his definition of the
subject matter of his brand of economics. "We may define
an institution as collective action in control, liberation and
expansion of individual action." [5]

TRANSACTIONS

These individual actions, Commons notes, are really *transactions* instead of purely individual behavior or a simple

---

[5] "Institutional Economics," *American Economic Review*, XXI (December, 1931), 651.

exchange of commodities. The economy is in fact a myriad of going concerns, bound together internally and related externally by a complex of working rules governing their interactions. One may, and Commons did, conceive of the going concern and the collective economy as a continuing and repetitive "flow of transactions."

The *transaction* thus becomes one of the building-block concepts in his more embracing concept of collective action. He regards it as the lowest common denominator of all economic activity, the elemental unit from which the whole edifice must be constructed. In the transaction are joined the three inescapable social relationships of conflict of interests (arising out of scarcity), interdependence of interests (arising out of the need for exchange), and order (or compromise, arising out of the need for establishing a system of working rules and expectations as the basis for exchange). Scratch any economic relationship, he says in effect, and you will find that it is based on a transaction which involves all three of these elements. In contrast to received economic doctrine, which had emphasized the product or the good as the basic building block, or an individual's pleasure-pain sentiments regarding it, Commons took his cue from the courts, where economic decisions start with a conflict of interests between transactors which has to be resolved by an appeal to social rules.

Commons distinguishes three types of transactions—bargaining, rationing, and managerial. A bargaining transaction is the negotiation between individuals of roughly equal status, who have alternatives open to them, of the terms on which ownership will be transferred. Although I am not sure he makes this explicit, bargaining transactions would logically, within his analytical framework, also seem to include negotiated agreements as to the way in which property may be used, even if title is not actually transferred. The essence of bargaining transactions is that they are voluntary, representing an agreement between people with more or less equal rights and privileges exercising no more coercion or duress than is sanctioned by the working rules of the society.

Rationing transactions are a substitute for bargaining transactions, for they too transfer ownership or amend property rights. They are a means of redistributing scarcity values. But they differ in being based on an authoritative rather than a voluntary relationship, one between a legal superior and a legal subordinate. The legal superior is a collective one—the government, a trade union, a board of directors. When a legislature allocates the tax burden, this is a rationing transaction. When a collective bargaining conference decides on the wage structure of a company, this is a rationing transaction as far as the individual workers are concerned. When a company draws up its budget, it rations among its departments and divisions.

Managerial transactions are also of a superior-subordinate nature, but these are the production decisions which follow the bargaining or rationing. They involve the organized use of the property or assets over which command has been acquired. Once the wage is set, the manager or foreman has the authority to command the services of the worker; title to his labor has been transferred, within the limitations and restrictions which society has imposed on the appropriate uses which may be made of it. Once the budget has been determined or tax revenues apportioned among the departments of a government, the managers have authority to conduct and direct the operations of their units by issuing appropriate orders to their subordinates.

Let us relate the two fundamental concepts which we have encountered so far: the all-embracing notion of collective action, and the building-block element of the transaction. Commons is saying that collective action (as we have identified it) determines all the economic relations of individuals. It does this in several ways:

Indirectly, by establishing the working rules which govern the bargaining relations between people, which establish the permissible limits of coercion and duress which individuals and organizations may bring to bear on each other.

Directly, by sanctioning certain rationing devices for allocating such scarcity-values as have not been distributed by bargaining. All governmental tax and expenditures programs are included in this category, as well as the decisions of going concerns like corporations and labor unions. It is the exercise of sovereignty and such bits of sovereignty as the state may have parcelled out to particular institutions.

Indirectly, by establishing the working rules on which the production processes go forward through the managerial direction by some of the work of others. This is an exercise of power obtained as a result of bargains or rations and can be traced back to proprietary rights. It is the shape of these rights which collective action affects.[6]

The distribution of economic goods depends on the way in which collective action affects these three types of transactions, which collectively exhaust all kinds of economic activity.

The mix of the three types of transactions changes with time and place. All three coexist in any society, but the degree to which one or another dominates affects the complexion of the society. Commons considered the growth in the size of the corporation in the United States as enlarging the sphere of rationing and managerial transactions and reducing the scope of bargaining transactions— a substitution of authority for discretion. Cross-culturally, he viewed the rise of communism and fascism as emphasizing the command and obedience relationships of the au-

---

[6] Summary of Commons's position.

thoritative rationing and managerial transactions, in contrast to the liberalistic economies of the West which still left important scope for choice and discretion in bargaining transactions. "But there may be all degrees of combinations, for the three kinds of transactions are interdependent and variable in a world of collective action and perpetual change which is the uncertain future world of institutional economics." [7]

THE VOLITIONAL ELEMENT IN ECONOMIC ACTIVITY

But what gives rise to transactions? Commons rejected the notion that these owe their origin to some common individualistic motivation operating as a natural force, like energy. "Self-interest" or "utility" were concepts too simplistic to be considered determinants of economic behavior. "The early nineteenth century economists patterned their work upon the materialistic sciences of physics and chemistry, instead of on a volitional science of the human will as developed by the courts. According to the materialists, the human individual acted somewhat like an atom, or like a natural law, and only in the one direction of overcoming the resistance of nature's forces in the production of wealth." [8] To Commons, with his eye on collective action, this atomistic pushing and pulling of individuals by some abstract force was an unsatisfactory explanation of human conduct. Purpose and "willingness"—volition—were to be found not only in the individual but also in his organized activity.

This notion of purpose—individual, organizational, and social—led Commons to distinguish the methodology of

---

[7] *Institutional Economics*, p. 93.

[8] *Economics of Collective Action* (New York: Macmillan, 1950), p. 36.

the social sciences from that of the physical sciences, or, in terms which he sometimes employed, the methodology of volitional theory from that of behavioristic theory. "A behavioristic theory takes account of *all* the factors of a moving mechanism . . . , and endeavors to ascertain the part played by each factor in producing the total behavior observed, without regard to any purpose or force that may be supposed to guide the behavior towards any given direction. A behavioristic theory, in other words, is physical science. It reaches its terminus when all the moving factors of a mechanism can be stated in terms of numbers and equations." [9]

Commons goes on to observe that this "mathematical agnosticism," as he labels it, is also the goal of some schools of psychology and sociology, and of those economists as well who emphasize statistical observation in the forms of leads and lags and the like, which can be reduced to formulas which describe the behavior of prices. "Economics becomes, like astronomy and physics, a set of numbers and equations which we call the movement of prices, found valid by the test of experiment, and all science is reduced to numerical terms without assumptions of cause and effect, purpose and instrument. . . ." [10]

Even those economists who had sought to introduce an evolutionary element into their subject matter had been overly influenced, Commons felt, by an attempted imitation of the physical sciences. He criticized Veblen on this score. Just as the exponents of a static physical equilibrium approach to economics had treated men as mechanistically subject to natural forces, so those, like Veblen, who had argued for an evolutionary approach had nevertheless thought in terms of a Darwinian *natural* selection. "The theorists of each stage attempted to get rid of the human

[9] *Legal Foundations of Capitalism* (New York: Macmillan, 1924), p. 374.
[10] *Ibid.*, p. 375.

will and to explain economic phenomena as the working out of natural forces, either foreordained or blind. It was a concept of society as the natural growth of a mechanistic equilibrium." [11]

On this score Commons stood in respect to Veblen (or at least his interpretation of Veblen) as Julian Huxley to Charles Darwin. Man has capabilities, in his *own* nature, of controlling the natural forces around him, and in this sense survival of institutions, just as of species, is at least partially subject to his control. Man can adapt his environment to his own needs and purposes. This implies purpose —volition, again to use Commons's special term—and substitutes what he called an "artificial selection" for the natural selection of the prehuman stages of development.

The end result, the "artificial mechanism," is not so much an equilibrium (a term Commons considered more appropriate to the physical world) as a social order infused with purpose and subject to continuing tinkering to effect that purpose more completely. "Thus a volitional or economic theory starts with the *purpose* for which the artificial mechanism in question was designed. . . . Then it inquires whether the artificial mechanism in question accomplishes that purpose in an efficient or economical way, and, if not, what is the limiting factor, out of the thousands of cooperating factors, that obstructs the operation, and to what extent that limiting factor can be, and requires to be, controlled in order to facilitate the mechanism and accomplish its purpose." [12]

This point of view brings us to an important characteristic of Commons's approach. If his institutional economics can be called a theory, it is an *operating* theory, combining analytical and normative aspects, in the best traditions of the profession. He says, in effect: Let's start with the no-

[11] *Ibid.*, p. 376.
[12] *Ibid.*, p. 377.

tion of purpose. Actually, we intrude this purpose onto a society already functioning through numerous going concerns, with a complex of working rules which they have built up for themselves. We are not so much interested in exploring in comprehensive detail *all* the transactions which take place and the rules which structure them. That would be a monumental task more appropriate to the study of a natural world where phenomenal relationships are more reduceable to generalization and stay put for longer periods of time. As long as social relationships are functioning reasonably satisfactorily, through a maze of routine or cooperating or complementary transactions which form the solid structure of society, the social scientist need not concern himself with these. He should set himself the more manageable and operationally significant task of identifying those particularly strategic transactions or relationships which, at this point in time, prevent the realization of social objectives. These Commons calls the "limiting factors."

If one thinks, for the moment, of the total economy as a mechanism, then it is the imperfect functioning of particular strategic or limiting factors which prevents the mechanism from performing as well as is wanted. One does not, then, concern oneself with the mechanism as a whole, which is puttering along reasonably well under its working rules; one attends to those aspects of the social machine which are not functioning properly because the working rules governing the relevant transactions are inadequate or just wrong. Because the generality is operating relatively well, we can concentrate on the particular relationships which are not.

In other words, volitionalism implies both purpose and concentration on the strategic obstacles to its achievement. It distinguishes between the complementary factors (routine transactions) and the limiting factors (inhibitors of goal achievement). "From a behavioristic standpoint many thousands, even millions of factors, must be taken into account in order to explain the phenomena of political economy, all the way from stars to atoms. But from the volitional standpoint, at any particular moment or circumstance, the economist, and indeed also the psychologist, deals with what for him is the set of limiting factors in accomplishing the further purpose which he deems worth while." [13]

This volitional approach applies at the level of the organization and of society as a whole. In a business, management presumably searches out the strategic factors which are preventing the firm from achieving its target position and operates on these. In society as a whole, it is presumably the governmental officials who assume this responsibility.

FUTURITY

It will be recalled that John R. Commons had set out in his first theoretical treatise in 1924 to construct a theory of value. The "theory" which resulted he has himself variously dubbed as one of "volitional value," "expectational value," and "reasonable value," thereby emphasizing three of the main conceptual constituents even if introducing at the same time that element of confusion which his penchant for varying nomenclature almost guaranteed. There have been few economists who have been so given to classification, subclassification, reclassification, and overclassification as Commons. Sets and categories of concepts parade through the pages of his two principal works, and it is not always easy to determine the functional relationships

---

[13] *Ibid.*, p. 378.

among them, their relative importance, and sometimes, indeed, their significance. But one element whose importance is clear, and which is related to his concept of expectational value, is futurity.

As he recites in his autobiography, *Myself,* it was his early work on public utility regulation in Wisconsin that first brought home to him the idea, "thrilling to me at that time, of legal valuations in economics as always looking toward the future. From this starting point I worked for many years in making Futurity the main principle of economics, distinguished from all the schools of economic thought which based their theories on past law or present feelings." [14]

The notion of futurity takes its logical origins from a very simple distinction, so simple that most economists had taken it for granted—the distinction between the thing itself and ownership of the thing. The thing itself may have scarcity value in a physical sense, but it takes a property right to endow it with institutional scarcity. The stolen object is no less scarce for being stolen rather than purchased, but in a going society it acquires economic meaning only when a transfer of title has been legalized. Legal possession must thus anticipate actual use, and bargains over legal possession must be based on expected values at the future time when the thing's use value or exchange value will actually be realized. Negotiations are always designed to put a present value on the legal claim to the expected future values to which the good will give rise.

Putting a value on future use may involve no trick with respect to the consumer goods items which are the subject of so many routine bargaining transactions. The goods which will be put to immediate use will undergo little change in value in the time elapsing between transfer of

---

[14] *Myself,* p. 125.

title and consumption. But the principle takes on greater importance with respect to negotiations for the present control of future production or production facilities. Here one encounters, for example, the question of prices fluctuating with supply and demand conditions changing in ways which can only be surmised. Will the labor which is hired for production now be worth, in the form of finished goods to be disposed of some months from now, as much as it cost? Will the capital equipment which is ordered for delivery in a year, on a firm-price contract, be worth its price when delivered, or will it be worth less, either because prices will have declined both with respect to the capital equipment itself and the products it is designed to make, or because more productive equipment will then be obtainable at the same price? The price which is negotiated now, in all such cases, depends on expectations of future values.

Negotiation for control of a going concern involves even more complications, since here the expected values are based in part on intangible property factors such as goodwill or special position. How much is a reputation or a brand name worth, for example? Whenever a company is sold for more than the cost of reproducing its facilities, a special consideration has been given to its value as a going concern. The distinction and respect which a firm has attached to its product or to its business dealings help to shield it from sharp competition, on the one hand, or to make it a more effective competitor, on the other, and in either case constitutes a genuine increment to its assets. The future stream of values to which it is expected to give rise is determined by something more than its goods-producing capacity. Commons was fond of pointing out that the price which Carnegie extracted for his steel company from the Morgan interests, when the latter merged it into the U. S. Steel Corporation, was many times what it would have cost to have built a mill of the same capacity. The additional value was an estimation of the future value to be derived by eliminating this source of low-priced competition. The cause of present value is the expected event of the future. The future determines the present, or, as Commons liked to put it somewhat enigmatically, the effect precedes the cause:

An expectation of bad markets six months or a year from now will cause securities and pig iron to fall in prices now. . . . The whole theory of economic causation is thus reversed in two respects. Instead of predetermined physical 'effective' causes coming up from the past and embodied in the present, it is a theory of indeterminate teleological 'final' causes coming back from the speculative future but also effective in the present. And instead of causation being something that inherently compels phenomena to occur, causation is merely a statistical statement of lags, forecasts, and probabilities.[15]

REASONABLENESS

As we have seen, scarcity and a resulting conflict of interests are Commons's basic economic premises. Scarcity finds its expression in society in property title, and competition between individuals and groups takes the form of negotiations over the terms on which title will be transferred (except in those situations where legal authority determines the issue by rationing transactions). Property ownership involves the power to withhold goods or services from the use of others, a power which can be employed to win concessions as to terms of exchange. This is a mutual power: both buyer and seller are in a position to withhold something the other wants and to conclude agree-

---

[15] J. R. Commons, H. L. McCracken, and W. E. Zeuch, "Secular Trends and Business Cycles: A Classification of Theories," *Review of Economic Statistics*, IV (October, 1922) , 262–263.

ments with alternative buyers and sellers on more favorable terms.

As long as people bring this element of bargaining power to their transactions, the question will inevitably be raised as to whether their exercise of it is "reasonable." Despite the importance of the concept of bargaining power in Commons's scheme of things, he did not spend much time dissecting it. He noted that it took the form of physical, economic, and moral sanctions, these being usually appropriate to the roles, respectively, of state, property, and church. But he did not go much beyond this. Certainly the attention he paid to the concept did not begin to compare to that lately lavished on it by everyone from game theorists to international specialists. For him, the essential thing was that the line between reasonable and unreasonable exercises of power was not drawn by any broad social philosophy or public principle but was hammered out on a case-by-case basis, in the resolution of particular disputes. As conflict of interest emerged, and protests were voiced over the unreasonable use of power by some offended person or group, the appropriate authority—a manager, an arbitrator, a court—would make a decision as to the merits of the complaints, and out of these decisions there would gradually cumulate a body of custom and law imposing limitations on the exercise of power. The rights of property, over which the economic contest takes place, become defined over time by an encrustation of working rules, court decisions, and traditions.

Bargaining power, Commons felt, can never be made equal between people or groups. But limits can be set to its exercise. These rights, privileges, powers, and immunities of property can be spelled out by judicial-like decisions, which become precedents, and whose total net effect is to move individuals and groups into reasonable relations with each other, bringing order out of conflict.

But what of the argument that there is no objective criterion of reasonableness, that what is reasonable is anybody's opinion? "This is the usual objection raised against a theory of reasonable value. There are as many individual opinions of reasonableness as there are individuals, just as there are as many opinions of what is pleasurable or painful as there are individuals." But this problem is, for Commons, readily amenable to solution. In the event of disputes over interests, custom could be given precision by some authoritative decision by an arbitrator, an executive, a board, or—and this to him was crucial—"finally, [by] the courts of law up to the Supreme Court of the United States." [16] After private decision has failed to resolve an issue, the judicial authority of the state would resolve the question, and ultimately the Supreme Court. For Commons the Supreme Court held a special position in the economic order. It was, indeed, his *deus in machina.* "Reasonable value is the *Court's* decision of what is reasonable as between plaintiff and defendant. It is objective, measurable in money, and compulsory." [17]

The ultimate sanction of the law, this final authority of the courts, helps to explain Commons's insistence that a useful theory of value must weave together economics, ethics, and the law. Economics arises in the form of scarcity-values based on a distribution of property. The fact of scarcity necessitates exchange transactions, invoking competition over the terms of agreement. The basis of competition is the power resident in property rights to withhold the goods and services from another's use, but the very existence of this power raises questions concerning its reasonable use. This is an ethical, not an economic question.

---

[16] *Institutional Economics,* p. 72.
[17] "Institutional Economics," *American Economic Review,* XXVI (March, 1936, Supp.), 244. (My italics.)

The question is best answered by the parties themselves: ". . . reasonableness is best ascertained in practice when representatives of conflicting organized economic interests, instead of politicians or lawyers, agree voluntarily on the working rules of their collective action in control of individual action." [18] But even agreement, when it is based on relative power positions, can hardly be given an ethical standing if there is not the possibility available to all, of an appeal to some objective authority as to the reasonableness of the methods employed to reach the results obtained. Otherwise, "agreement" may be only the surrender of the weak to the strong and unscrupulous. Bargaining power cannot be equalized, but people can be given equal access to the law for such a determination when their sense of justice is outraged. Ultimately, then, questions of the exercise of power, of the rights of property, funnel up to the highest judicial authority in the land, which passes on their reasonableness. Economic values, scarcity-values, which have been validated by this process are then *reasonable values.* Establishing valuation on scarce goods and services, the determination of prices, is not something arising out of an equilibrium of human atoms, but by the purposive transactions of many individuals and groups within a setting of law and custom whose ultimate arbiter (of both purpose and method) is the High Court. Thus economics, ethics, and law combine to create a system of reasonable values.

With Veblen, who reasoned from the shrewd and sometimes crude transactions of unregulated business, a large ingredient of institutionalism was the private search for exploitative devices. To Commons, who reasoned from the transactions of groups as limited by custom and the courts, the largest ingredient of institutionalism was the collective determination of how much bargaining power (that is, ex-

---

[18] *Economics of Collective Action,* p. 25.

ploitative power) was consistent with the purposes and objectives of organizations and society as a whole. Commons is saying that Veblen's notion of private exploitation is valid up to the point where society, through intermediaries such as arbitrators and courts, passes on the reasonableness of such actions, laying down guidelines which become precedents or rules. But at that point whatever exercise of bargaining power is permitted becomes taken into the vast body of institutional procedures and practices governing the vast body of routine, complementary transactions out of which prices get set and values are made reasonable.

COMMONS'S INSTITUTIONALISM AND ECONOMIC THEORY

Commons has often been distinguished from other institutionalists by his preoccupation with conceptualization. If others of the "school" were given to writing industry studies or union histories, for Commons the important thing about these was that they constituted the raw data from which concepts could be built. In this sense he was an abstract economist. It would be stretching a point, however, to speak of him as a theorist. If he is intent on conceptualization, he shows little interest in—perhaps even some aversion to—knitting those concepts into a system of thought. Commons's institutionalism is more a way of looking at economic activity and structuring it broadly than an effort to build generalizations with predictive value. One of his graduate students quotes him as having remarked in a class lecture, "I have no system. I have an administrative process." [19]

---

[19] From a dissertation by Leona Spilman, cited by Joseph Dorfman in *The Economic Mind in American Civilization*, Vol. 4 (New York: Viking Press, 1959), p. 390.

In only a slight oversimplification it could be said that Commons concentrated on what he conceived to be the basic unit of the economy, the transaction, looking, as it were, through a microscope, and that he then used a telescope to look at the all-embracing concept of collective action. But he was largely disinterested in any theory which would relate functionally the two objects of his vision. In his concept of the bargaining transaction he wedded Davenport's notion of opportunity cost (alternatives) to his own preoccupation with the judicial review of the reasonableness of coercive powers, thus arriving at the concept of reasonable value. But he made little effort to fit this (or his rationing and managerial transactions) within a systematic framework. Admittedly, he did not seek to examine the determinants of wants (except as he lumps them broadly under a "volitional psychology" or relegates them to the hedonic values of the "home" economists) , nor does he explore the nature of "alternatives." He showed little interest in analyzing how his basic unit, the transaction, was compounded into the complex of activity which we identify as the economy. In short, Commons was a concept builder but not a system builder.

Why this should have been so has several possible explanations. One is especially worth considering, more because of its relevance to the whole conception of social studies as a science than because it is idiosyncratic to Commons, the individual. Commons looked on individuals not as discrete economic units connected only by price transactions but as parts of organizations and institutions, each with its own (sometimes confused) objectives, seeking to achieve these by manipulating whatever power society permits it to exercise. The objectives are not always —perhaps are seldom—compatible, and no single principle can lead to a determinate result. Common's own major "connecting" principle was "volitionalism," which works out to a kind of transient balance of pressures and sanctions within society. In this view, individual and group objectives (right on up to the largest group, the nation) are satisfied as far as possible and permissible by compromise with other individuals and groups. The basis for agreement is power, restrained "within reason" by a set of working rules.

But this volitional "principle" is indeterminate. The working rules can change, the composition of organizations can change, their power base can change, their objectives can change—all in relatively unpredictable ways. One could and must seek to identify likely responses to such changes, but the range of possible resulting activity is limited only by the imagination and perseverance of people operating within a framework over which they themselves have some measure of control. No "natural" or "expectable" equilibrium is involved.

Such "equilibrium" as exists is not automatic. It must be contrived and controlled; it is equivalent, simply, to social order, the continuity in the economic system. The system of transactions is governed by a complex of customs and rules which people, collectively, in private and public organizations, can *will* to modify, rules which are always subject to the pulling and hauling of variable power relationships and variable purposes.

From this point of view, Commons accepted as "given" the mass of the existing set of institutions and customs and going concerns, and the routine, complementary transactions taking place within them. This, which to the general economic theorist is the system which requires explanation, is the system which to him required none. But the disputes and issues and explosive points and problem areas—the limiting factors which to the general theorist are likely to be swept under the rug as "frictions"—these were the things which to Commons called for probing and for new solutions.

How then should we evaluate the work of this rugged individualist who was in love with collective action, this combination reformer and conceptualist, rooted in the soil of the Middle West but easily transplantable to the faster industrializing East, this economist whom Wesley Mitchell once called, in a complimentary way, "a bewildering person"? Why does Commons stand out on the economic landscape? What distinguishes him from the hundreds of his contemporary co-workers who were writing on the same topics which occupied him?

Commons's intense interest is probably one distinguishing feature of his importance. Moreover, in describing the American economy in conceptual terms that contribute to our understanding of it, he achieved a degree of generality that rose above the case study—which standing by itself fails to reveal in what respects it is similar to other cases and in what respects unlike. He was, indeed, far from the caricature of the institutionalist, the writer of histories of particular institutions. He was a concept builder, a generalist who believed, distinguishingly, that concepts, as abstractions, had to abstract from something. That something was the real-life activity of a society. He grubbed for details, not to report them untreated or unrefined, but in order to extract from them the elements which gave them larger significance. His abstract concepts were thus founded in observation and experience, not in introspection and *a priori* surmise.

His persistent pragmatism led him to ask again and again: *How* do our economic institutions work, and *why* do they work? He was not interested, as Veblen was, in debunking. He was no muckraker of economic theory who delighted in demonstrating theoretical fallacies and the cultural predispositions and special-interest biases which may have led to them. Commons operated more like a cultural anthropologist. He found a society whose economic institutions were obviously working to achieve particular results. Those results were not imposed by some natural force outside the system, nor were they willed by something which might be called "the system itself." They were the outcome of the wills of numbers of people seeking their own ends through compromise with numbers of other people doing likewise.

Looking at such a system—never in equilibrium, always in motion, always going somewhere—Commons sought to describe in general terms the parts of the process by which the numerous compromises which were its objectives (volitional values) took the form of transactions through the medium of its institutions, its going concerns, and its collective rules. These did not add up to some grand design; they were pragmatic and contrived results.

There was, of course, one peculiar unifying force to which he gave a special place—the U. S. Supreme Court. It was the Supreme Court which passed on all the efforts of people and institutions to achieve their special interests, to use coercive power in place of persuasion. Coercion could not be avoided, but society could impose limits to its exercise. But "society" was too big an abstraction for Commons to swallow. A decision as to what was acceptable or unacceptable had to be traced to the real live beings who made it. For Commons these were the judges of the Supreme Court, who functioned as the conscience and codifier of the American people.

It is easy enough to find ground for criticizing this economist's product. His verbal prolixity and complexity often obscured his meaning, as he himself was painfully aware. His penchant for classification and categorization may sometimes have led him to make distinctions which were not essential, or which could be subsumed under a more embracing concept, or which may even have obscured his intent. As reasonable as his threefold classification of transactions appears on the surface, it is difficult to work with in practice, and I am uneasy at his apparent willingness to eliminate the bargaining element from the rationing and managerial transactions. As is so often the case with intellectual innovators, he had a fixation which was a source of both strength and weakness, namely, his preoccupation with the legal basis for economic activity. He valuably focused attention on this neglected component of economic analysis, but he did so with an emphasis that contributed distortions of its own. His insistent distinction between use-value and scarcity-value often leads him down prickly bypaths, away from his main trail.

But let me conclude on an affirmative note, by indicating what I believe to be the major contributions of this sifting mind. To some extent they are to be found in the concepts which if he did not originate he helped to establish. We inevitably associate with him the notion of the transaction, and especially the bargained transaction. We link the idea of the going concern with him as well as with Veblen. We credit him, again along with Veblen, with delineating the concept of intangible property and of defining present worth as being the sum of discounted future (expected) values.

In the area of methodology he helped to establish, as did his teacher Ely before him, the importance of field investigation. Through his workshop technique, which enlisted the collaboration of his graduate students, and in his industrial investigations he stressed the need for organized research, asserting in a paper prepared in 1938 for the Social Science Research Council that "the social sciences of the future must be large-scale university research bureaus, as well as training laboratories for beginners." Perhaps out of his infatuation with the common law he laid great stress on the comparative method, the "method of similarities and differences," as the basis for scientific investigation.

But it is not in the areas of specific concepts or methodological techniques that I find Commons's greatest contribution to the economic profession which he so revered. It lies in the realm of what, for want of a better term, I shall simply call naked insights. Often expressed with courage in the face of criticism and misunderstanding, they permeated his thinking. He helped to keep alive, in an age moving towards an opposite sentiment, the insight that economics, since it is always teleological with respect to man, can never constitute an exact science. Hence the human will must always be an important part of economics. This may be studied objectively, scientifically, but it cannot be built into a predictable system. Along with the large element of continuity and order, which by and large can be ignored, there are inescapable areas of disorder and discontinuity, which must be resolved by human wills. The most important of these are the strategic factors limiting social achievement. The objective is to use creative intelligence in moving these from the category of the strategic and limiting to the category of the routine and complementary.

His second great insight was of the pervasiveness of collective activity, both in the form of organization and in custom. If every individual were like an isolated atom, and each subject to the same forces, perhaps some Walrasian general equilibrium could indeed be posited. But when individuals join with each other to form associations, build cliques within them, split into factions, divide into competing and coöperating societies, contest over the rules which should limit or release their behavior—then the possibility is ruled out of automatic individual adjustment of the inevitable conflicts to which scarcity gives rise. Agreement must be contrived, bargained out at many levels, and this process becomes an integrally important aspect of all of economics, not a specialized and rather unimportant field tucked away under the rubric of industrial relations.

These two insights are still worth pondering. If many of the particulars of Commons's thinking have been outdated or seem invalid, at times perhaps even naïve, the underlying message still comes through—perhaps with even greater force and relevance in a day when so many economists are prone to emphasize the mathematical relationship of the parts in a way that ignores volitional qualities or bargaining relationships. On the other hand, those economists who are working with simulation techniques, bargaining relationships, game theory, and the like, are probably more nearly in the Commons tradition. They too are likely to find difficulty in fitting their developing concepts into a viable theoretical system. They too are likely to be thrown back upon some fundamental questions which make us all uneasy, in part because they seem to jeopardize the status of our profession, in part because they leave us wondering what knowledge is possible. How detailed can prediction get when conflicting human wills are involved and bargains must be struck even to assure continuity and order? What is the meaning of equilibrium under these circumstances? How necessary is prediction to a science, and how applicable is prediction to economics?

Questions like these always need raising. But they are not often raised, out of fear that eyebrows will arch. It takes the inner simplicity (even if not the verbal complexity) of a John R. Commons to spend his life asking and trying to give answer to them.

FOUR

The Contribution of
Wesley C. Mitchell

Some thirteen years have elapsed since the death of Wesley Clair Mitchell in October 1948; and less than a decade has gone by since the publication of a volume dealing in some detail with his life and work.[1] But with the accelerated pace of history and marked shifts in the identity of problems that occupy economists, much has happened during these few years. I welcome the invitation to attempt in a brief discussion to restate Wesley Mitchell's contribution —as it is seen today by one who has been, and still is, his student and follower.

I shall begin by summarizing Mitchell's basic views on the role and task of economics, then go on to indicate how Mitchell's extensive work in the field represented an application of these views in the circumstances of his life, to appraise the cumulative impact of his work and of the work of others that it inspired, and, in conclusion, shall consider whether the value of Mitchell's basic views in developing a valid and useful body of economic knowl-

---

[1] Arthur F. Burns, ed., *Wesley Clair Mitchell: The Economic Scientist* (New York: National Bureau of Economic Research, 1952) .

edge has been impaired or enhanced by the changes that have occurred in the discipline and in the world since his death.

Like all major economists, Mitchell had to formulate his position on the doctrinal heritage from his predecessors—particularly that embodied in general theory for which acceptance was claimed. A searching appraisal of such established theory has always been needed in economics because, by admission, this body of doctrine was not based on testable evidence but, at best, on highly plausible assumptions concerning human nature and its economic rationality under rigorously specified and oversimplified conditions.

One basic view in Mitchell's general outlook was his recognition of the serious limitations of the accepted economic theory of his day—not as to consistency, but as to content. During the decade of the twenties many of his articles on the general framework of the economic discipline appeared. In dealing with "The Prospects of Economics," in 1924, by which time his views were fully matured, he both noted the basic shortcomings and referred to the "fresh fields" that the impact of events and progress in related disciplines would have on "the economist's demesne":

It will become evident that orthodox economic theory, particularly in the most clarified recent types, is not so much an account of how men do behave as an account of how they would behave if they followed out in practice the logic of the money economy. Now the money economy, seen from the new viewpoint, is in fact one of the most potent institutions in our whole culture. In sober truth it stamps its pattern upon wayward human nature, makes us all react in standard ways to the standard stimuli it offers, and affects our very ideals of what is good, beautiful, and true. The strongest testimony to the power and pervasiveness of this institution in molding human behavior is that a type of economic theory that implicitly assumed men to be perfectly disciplined children of the money economy could pass for several generations as a social science. The better orientation we are getting will not lead economists to neglect pecuniary logic as a sterile or an exhausted field. On the contrary, not only will it make clear the limitations of the older work, but it will also show how the old inquiries may be carried further, and how they may be fitted into a comprehensive study of economic behavior.[2]

Given this limitation of accepted economic theory to a close analysis of the logic of the money economy, founded on restrictive assumptions concerning rationality of human nature, Mitchell's second basic view is the need to widen it to "a comprehensive study of economic behavior." And this means focusing "our attention . . . upon the role played in behavior by institutional factors." " 'Institutions' is merely a convenient term for the more important among the widely prevalent, highly standardized social habits" which mold the rather plastic human behavior and yield its different patterns through history, although "our reflexes, instincts, and capacity to learn are believed to be substantially the same as those of our cave-dwelling ancestors." And finally, "of course, it is mass behavior that the economist studies. Hence, the institutions that standardize the behavior of men create most of the openings for valid generalizations. That was true even of Ricardian economics, when the generalizations were made by the treacherous method of reasoning on the basis of imputed economic motives." [3]

The emphasis on institutions in the study of economic

---

[2] See "The Prospects of Economics," in R. G. Tugwell, ed., *The Trend of Economics* (New York: Knopf, 1924) ; reprinted in Wesley C. Mitchell, *The Backward Art of Spending Money and Other Essays* (New York: McGraw-Hill, 1937) , p. 371. Further quotations from this source will refer to *BASM*.

[3] *Ibid.*, pp. 372–375 *passim*.

behavior is clearly due to their mutability over time and the resulting differences in institutional patterns coexisting at any given time. The evolutionary character of institutions—their gradual formation, maturity, and decay—is clearly recognized whenever we study them realistically. Even the pecuniary economy developed gradually and unevenly; and the excogitation of its complicated logic as a highly developed and consistent type, while useful, necessarily reflects the concentration on a case at one point in a vast range. The emphasis on institutions means, therefore, in the first place an emphasis on change. Furthermore, since a variety of institutions are always in operation, some more dominant than others, some waxing and others waning in scope and power, a realistic comprehensive study of economic behavior should deal with this multiplicity. If, as a result of deliberate choice arising out of a scholar's interest or concern with methodological feasibility, this is not done, we must be aware of the limited application in time and space (and hence to "institutions") of the resulting analysis and generalizations.

Third, emphasis on the study of mass economic behavior, in changing and diverse institutional conditions, led Mitchell to advocate and insist upon the quantitative, statistical approach. Already in 1918, in his presidential address to the American Statistical Association, in discussing the future usefulness of the social sciences, he wrote:

The social sciences, however, cover an immense field, and it is not probable that we shall encounter failure or success in all its parts. The parts where effort seems most promising just now are the parts in which this Association is particularly interested. Measurement is one of the outstanding characteristics of science at large, whether in the field of inorganic matter or that of life processes. Social statistics, which is concerned with the measurement of social phenomena, has many of the progressive features of the physical sciences. It shows forthright progress in knowledge of fact, in technique of analysis, and in refinement of results. It is amenable to mathematical formulation. It is objective. A statistician is usually either right or wrong, and his successors can demonstrate which. Statisticians are not continually beginning their science all over again by developing new viewpoints. Where one investigator stops, the next investigator begins with larger collections of data, with extensions into fresh fields, or with more powerful methods of analysis. In all these respects, the position and prospects of social statistics are more like the position and prospects of the natural sciences than like those of the social sciences.[4]

Six years later, in his presidential address to the American Economic Association, Mitchell again dealt significantly with quantitative analysis, this time specifically with regard to economic theory, pointing to the growth of statistics and their increased use in economic study as a hopeful basis for more realistic theory:

. . . the increase in statistical data, the improvement of statistical technique, and the endowment of social research are enabling economists to make a larger use of quantitative analysis; in preparing their work, the quantitative theorists usually find it necessary to formulate problems in a way different from that adopted by qualitative theorists; this technical necessity of restating problems promises to bring about radical changes in economic theory, in particular to make the treatment of behavior more objective, to emphasize the importance of institutions, and to promote the development of an experimental technique.[5]

And in "The Prospects of Economics," already quoted, after stressing the need to study mass behavior as patterned by institutions and referring to the "treacherous method of reasoning on the basis of imputed economic

---

[4] See "Statistics and Government," reprinted in *BASM*, p. 52.
[5] See "Quantitative Analysis in Economic Theory," reprinted in *BASM*, pp. 32–33.

motives" involved in Ricardian economics, Mitchell added:

> A much more dependable set of generalizations can be attained as rapidly as objective records of mass behavior become available for analysis. The extension and improvement of statistical compilations is, therefore, a factor of the first consequence for the progress of economic theory. Gradually economics will become a quantitative science. It will be less concerned with puzzles about economic motives and more concerned about the objective validity of the account it gives of economic processes.[6]

Fourth, as several passages cited above indicate, Mitchell hoped and expected that a growing recognition of the oversimplified views of human nature underlying accepted economic theory, an increasing attention to institutions and their patterning influence on economic behavior, and a wider use of statistics would lead to a reformulation of economic theory. His writings do not, as far as I know, indicate explicitly what such reformulated economic theory might be like. We may reasonably assume that the omission was deliberate, that Mitchell foresaw the process of its development as a drawn-out and gradual one for which he could, at the beginning, have no adequate basis for forecasting the end. Nor would he have thought of it as a determinate, fixed end: the process would be one of gradual revision and restatement, with shifts in emphasis and the development of new branches to deal with newly emerging problems.

Still, from his writings we can glean some aspects of the reformulation. For one thing, the concepts used in economic theory would have to be made operational, so that they would have counterparts, direct or indirect, in empirical study. The possible shifts in emphasis he indi-

[6] See *BASM*, pp. 375–376.

cated in his presidential address to the American Economic Assocation, when he stressed Veblen's thesis on the "relation between business and industry, between making money and making goods, between the pecuniary and the technological phases of economic life," [7] in "The Prospects of Economics," when he expected "the recession of the theory of value and distribution from the central position it has held ever since the days of Ricardo to make room for a theory of production," [8] and where he also wrote, "In becoming consciously a science of human behavior economics will lay less stress upon wealth and more stress upon welfare. Welfare will mean not merely an abundant supply of serviceable goods, but also a satisfactory working life filled with interesting activities." [9] And, finally, he indicated that there would be continuous testing not only by quantitative analysis, but in application to various policy problems. The reformulation would thus be a continuous process of interplay between hypotheses, data, and policy questions—with what Mitchell hoped would be increasing validity and hence increasing usefulness, but with no obvious and fixed end, no "true and only" theory for all times.

Fifth, and last, as has already become evident, to Mitchell economic theory and economic study were tools for society's intelligent and optimal adaptation to successive problems, a way of understanding the factors determining economic performance, and a basis for deliberate action to remove restrictions that accepted institutions might impose on technological and welfare potentials. It is for this reason that he stressed the contrast between pecuniary and technological aspects and hoped for the shift in economic theory toward an adequate theory of

---

[7] *Ibid.*, p. 29.

[8] *Ibid.*, p. 378.

[9] *Ibid.*, p. 381.

production. That this objective was fundamental to him
was evident as early as 1918 in a most eloquent passage in
his address to the American Statistical Association, written
with the impressions of the war fresh in his mind. In
urging further quantitative and statistical studies, not on
the *ad hoc* and feverish basis of wartime but in peacetime,
for better knowledge and more intelligent treatment of
social problems, he wrote:

> While I think that the development of social science offers
> more hope for solving our social problems than any other line
> of endeavor, I do not claim that these sciences in their present
> state are very serviceable. They are immature, speculative,
> filled with controversies. Their most energetic exponents are
> still in the stage of developing new 'viewpoints,' beginning
> over again on a different plan instead of carrying further the
> analysis of their predecessors. . . . In short, the social sciences
> are still children. Nor have we any certain assurance that they
> will ever grow into robust manhood, no matter what care we
> lavish upon them. There are blind leads of speculation in
> which past generations have mined industriously for ages with
> little gain. Perhaps the social sciences will prove more like
> metaphysics than like mechanics, more like theology than like
> chemistry. The race may always shape its larger destinies by a
> confused struggle in which force and fraud, good intentions,
> fiery zeal, and rule of thumb are more potent factors than
> measurement and planning. Those of us who are concerned
> with the social sciences, then, are engaged in an uncertain en-
> terprise. . . . But certainly it is our task to work out this lead
> with all the intelligence and the energy we possess until its
> richness or sterility be demonstrated.[10]

It is not possible here to discuss in adequate detail
Mitchell's writings or his activities as a teacher, as a guide
of organized research in economics, and as a collaborator
with scholars in other disciplines. The volume of papers

---

[10] *Ibid.*, p. 51.

referred to in footnote 1 provides this information and contains a variety of valuable appraisals. Let me then state my own impressions briefly.

Mitchell's writings (aside from brief reviews, notes, forewords, and the like), listed in the bibliography in that volume, fall into two distinct groups. The first, best known although not necessarily most read, covers the major empirical and statistical studies, dealing largely with far-reaching problems in the performance of the economy of this country. It includes the early studies of the greenback period during the Civil War, published over the period from 1897 to 1908; the studies of business cycles, from the classic monograph of 1913 to Volume I of the more elaborate undertaking in 1927, followed by *Measuring Business Cycles* (written jointly with Arthur F. Burns, in 1946), and the posthumous volume in 1951, supplemented intermittently by shorter papers on the subject; the monograph on index numbers of prices for the Bureau of Labor Statistics in 1915 and the studies of prices during World War I; and the masterly summary of the national income estimates published in Volume I of the first study by the National Bureau of Economic Research (in 1921). The concentration of these studies on money, prices, and business cycles, their unity in treating, with depth of observation, mastery of detail, and skill in organization, those aspects of the money economy that must be understood in gauging properly its short-term responses to long-term potentials is evident; and has been much commented upon. They are models of the kind of study that Mitchell saw as indispensable in providing a basis for a realistic and useful discipline of economics.

The second group includes a variety of papers dealing with broader aspects of economic theory and research, in which Mitchell stated his position along the lines discussed above or called attention to some aspects of human behavior neglected in economic analysis. It also includes lengthy reviews of some key contributions to economics, either in the days of Bentham and Ricardo or in the more recent days of Sombart, Wieser, Veblen, and Commons. And one should certainly mention his lectures on types of economic theory, delivered to large and attentive bodies of graduate students at Columbia University and recorded in two volumes of notes that Mitchell was never willing to revise and approve for publication. This body of essentially theoretical writings is in some respects equally as important as that of the major empirical studies, for it has reached a larger audience and possibly has affected the thinking of a wider body of scholars.

Perhaps it would be best to say that the two groups of his writings are complementary. The empirical studies revealed both the complexity and the intricate order of economic processes as they were observed and measured, demonstrated to the profession that much could be learned from systematic observations based on tested techniques, inhibited the formulation of theoretical hypotheses that rested upon simple notions of the behavior of money or of economic cycles, and stimulated the more satisfying if more difficult theorizing that could supply links among observed regularities. The theoretical writings, in rather brief articles, dealt directly with the broader methodological issues, analyzed the characteristics of past and current theories, and suggested the wider implications and promise of the kind of empirical research that was embodied in the larger substantive studies.

But Mitchell was not only a scholar and teacher; he was also an organizer—when forced to be by the inadequacy of the existing institutional conditions for the pursuit of the type of research that he felt was needed. Because of his conviction of the importance of quantitative analysis and the statistical approach, he became one of the founders of the National Bureau of Economic Research and devoted much of his time and energies to guiding that organization for a quarter of a century. Two aspects of Mitchell's association with the National Bureau are particularly to be noted. The first was his active participation and generous guidance in the studies prepared by other members of the staff, where he was *primus inter pares;* so that in a sense most of the Bureau's studies during his lifetime (and implicitly even after it) were an integral part of Mitchell's own scientific life work. His vision, interest, encouragement, and patience contributed significantly while the studies were in process; his reviews were generous but searching; his introductory or summary statements were always a valuable addition to the published monographs. Second, the distinctive features of the National Bureau's organization—the choice of topics, each of which dealt with some major quantitative aspect of the nation's economy; the conditions of work that facilitated a scholar's concentration on testable features of economic reality and left him free to explore them as best he could; the provisions for review by a board of directors including not only academic scholars but also men of affairs of varying affiliation, a review that permitted a director to add his observations if he felt so impelled but not to change the statements of the scholar responsible for the study; and, finally, the requirement that no policy recommendations be made—all of these were reflections of Mitchell's own views on the nature and conditions of objective realistic research in economics. I do not know whether Mitchell was the author of the by-laws of the National Bureau; but he participated in the discussions at the very beginning (brought in by Malcolm C. Rorty and N. I. Stone), and his long years of association in themselves bear testimony to his full agreement with the main features of the National Bureau's organization.

The requirement that policy recommendations be excluded, since they involve ethical and other considerations on which a scholar, as a scholar, has no particular claim to express judgments, was a fundamental tenet in Mitchell's outlook on the relation between science and policy. He held to it all the more strongly because he thought that much of economic writing in the past had suffered from a conflict between objectivity and reform zeal; and, I suspect, because he himself, interested as he was in the possible improvements of economy and society, was aware how strong the drive for reform is, and how easily it can produce bias in selecting and weighing evidence. A passage from his introduction to the annual report of the National Bureau, published on the occasion of the Bureau's twenty-fifth anniversary, elaborates this concern:

Our self-imposed rule against expressing opinions on public policy may be thought of as a corollary of our basic rule that the Board of Directors shall include men of differing views on social policy. Some feared that from an organization confining its efforts to the strictly scientific task of investigating what happens would come reports of slight interest and no practical value. Many a book on economics owes its effectiveness largely to trenchant criticism of abuses and moral fervor for reform. That these qualities are not necessarily incompatible with vigorous analysis is demonstrated by the *Wealth of Nations*, Mill's *Principles*, Marx's *Capital*, and Keynes' *General Theory*, not to mention the cloud of lesser witnesses. But the eager souls who think emotional drive and practical recommendations are essential to effectiveness in an economic book forget how the better established sciences have made their great contributions to human life. What these sciences have done is to explain in detail the operation of many processes. When men have learned what consequences must be expected from certain operations, they can choose those leading to consequences they prefer. Scientists who lament that the knowledge they have won is often applied to evil ends are no more effective preachers of righteousness than other men, and, like others, they frequently differ among themselves as to what consequences are good, what bad. Those who are trying to do scientific work in the peculiarly complex field of economics have no more and no less claim to set themselves up as ethical judges than chemists or physiologists. Their special competence is confined to the job of finding out as definitely as possible what happens under specified conditions. So far as they succeed, they enable all citizens, including themselves, to foresee consequences more clearly, and so to act more intelligently.[11]

Finally, Mitchell's concern with institutions made for a keen interest in social science disciplines other than economics and for an eagerness to participate in any undertaking that would facilitate effective cooperation among all social studies. He read intensively in anthropology, psychology, and related fields and taught courses that stressed the origin and early evolution of monetary institutions—as a young man in his twenties at the University of California. Later in life, he took an active part in the Social Science Research Council, an organization designed to promote cooperation among all social science disciplines, and engaged in a variety of collaborative activities that took him beyond the realm of economics proper. This roaming in other fields not only assured fuller recognition of the limitations of economics *per se;* it also gave him the opportunity to learn from students of other aspects of man and society and convey to them what economics could teach.

An attempt to make a summary appraisal of Mitchell's contribution must cope with several difficulties. There is, to begin with, some difficulty in distinguishing between

---

[11] Wesley C. Mitchell, "The National Bureau's First Quarter-Century," *Twenty-fifth Annual Report of the National Bureau of Economic Research* (New York, May 1945), p. 35.

the contribution of his writings, on the one hand, and, on the other, his major contribution as an inspiration to others through his personal example as an economic scientist as well as through his studies. There is, furthermore, the related question of how much of the contribution of Mitchell's colleagues and followers, in the cumulative impact of their work, should be credited to Mitchell —but for the fortune of having had him with us, much of that work might never have seen the light of day. My own preference is to consider the contributions of Mitchell and of his colleagues and followers as a collective enterprise. Finally, the development of economic research and analysis resulting from the work of Mitchell and his colleagues and students was a joint product of the interest that he inspired and the stimulus that he provided, and of the changing circumstances in this country and in the world at large. We face, therefore, a problem of specific imputation with, at least as far as I can see, no adequate tools. Yet with apology in advance for possible over- and understatement, let me try to summarize the contribution in several areas.

First, and most obvious, Mitchell contributed greatly to our knowledge of the functioning of the economy in this country and in other countries possessing a similarly developed money economy. His major empirical studies shed light on how money actually operates; on how the differential response of various groups in the economy tends to generate business cycles; on the general orders of magnitude involved in the aggregate performance of this country's economy. And the extensive monographic studies of his students and colleagues added to the wealth of tested data and analysis relating to the quantitative characteristics of economic change and the measured behavior of important sectors and institutions.

Second, the insistence on the use of statistical data and

the very attempts to use them consistently, comprehensively, and carefully, in application to clearly important economic questions and problems, had a cumulative impact on the collection of the underlying data by those institutions in our society (largely governments, but also some private collectives) with the power to do so on a sustained and adequate basis. Mitchell's work on prices, business cycles, and national income, supplemented by the work of his followers, prompted a vast extension of the basic statistical compilations in this country and, indirectly, in other countries. In many cases, Mitchell and his colleagues at the National Bureau directly stimulated statistical activity by government; their ideas and experiments were adopted by government agencies, with larger resources applied and wider scope and continuity assured. This happened to the work on price index numbers, national income, and capital formation, the flow of funds, consumer credit, and most recently business cycle indicators. And this extension of basic economic statistics by United States governmental agencies had its effect also in other countries, particularly after World War II. The impressive increase in the supply, continuity, and coverage of basic economic statistics the world over may thus be partly credited to the pioneering efforts of Mitchell and the followers whom he inspired.

Third, Mitchell's empirical studies, and those of his colleagues, had a quickening impact on economic theory. They tended to sharpen some of the concepts, in clear confirmation of Mitchell's expectation that the attempt to apply qualitative distinctions to empirical data would raise questions and call for reformulations that would not be apparent in either literary discussions or conventional mathematical model building. By attempts to secure their measurable counterparts with the help of statistical data, the concepts of money, price, profit, income, capital, industry, product, and the like were clarified and alternative variants were provided where significantly different meanings could be discerned. Furthermore, the substantive empirical findings—whether they related to leads, lags, degrees of conformity, or differences in amplitude in the participation of various economic activities in business cycles; to shifts in the relative weights of various industries or financial institutions in the country's economy in the course of time; or to the movements of national income and its significant components, in the business cycle or in the long run—affected profoundly and quickened the pace of theoretical work, largely in macro-economic theory but also to some extent even in the theory of the firm. This is only natural, for theorists are eager for observations of economic reality geared to adequately reformulated concepts and linked with partial hypotheses and the provision of such observations cannot but hasten the progress of theoretical analysis.

Fourth, Mitchell's views on the limitations of accepted economic theory, which he shared with Veblen and others of the institutionalist school, helped to weaken its hold and to lessen the dogmatic assurance with which it was preached, while preserving its most valuable elements. The insistence on the kernel of empirical content that every theory must contain; the revelation that theories could easily be elaborated, on the basis of preconceptions and postulates, to explain how a given economic process *could* be generated, whereas one that explained how in fact the process did occur was far more difficult; the realization of the extent to which much of economic theory was in direct response to the problems of the day and did not refer to a wider realm of experience—all these views of Mitchell helped his generation and his followers to examine accepted economic theory with critical and discerning eyes and to appraise it and its modern variants as plausible suggestions, relevant to some specific institutional framework of transient nature, rather than to treat them as fundamental truths or, even worse, empty tautology. This seems to me an important contribution, for nothing restricts the progress of a complex discipline like economics more than too facile an acceptance of general theory as truth just because it is logically consistent and plausible or too ready rejection of it as mere tautology or amateur effort at applied mathematics without empirical content or observational relevance.

Finally, Mitchell's view of the importance of realistic economic analysis as a basis of public policy contributed to a much more flexible conception of the possibilities of intelligent economic policy than might otherwise have been the case. I have already quoted from the 1918 address to the American Statistical Association in which he emphasized the importance of statistics for intelligent public policy. His own studies and those of his followers, by their very extension of the stock of tested knowledge concerning the operation of the country's economy, provided one of the tools of more active and intelligent public policy by governments and by other agencies. Such increased knowledge, combined with the loosening of the restrictive effects of accepted economic doctrine, provided an enriched background for specific consideration of specific data for specific policy problems, with constraints introduced only by what is firmly known, not by what is believed to be known, and perhaps by other grounds for choice beyond the sphere of economics proper. Thus, the additions to the stock of tested knowledge and the critical revaluation of accepted theory made for both more and better choices in public policy. This is obvious enough to require no further discussion.

But I would like to note, in this connection, that Mitchell was always willing to serve in the application of

tested knowledge to public policy; that his work during
World War I made him an eager advocate of the use of
economic data for economic policy—not just on an *ad hoc*
basis in wartime but in peacetime; that he was a member
of both the National Planning Board (in 1933) and the
National Resources Board (in 1934–35) ; and that in two
papers in the mid-thirties—his presidential address to the
American Association for the Advancement of Science and
his address at the Tercentenary Celebration at Harvard
University—he strongly advocated the formation of a national planning council that would continuously assemble
the results of tested social science research in order to
provide advice on social policy.[12]

The contributions of Mitchell's views and work as suggested may be overstated, for much of the expansion of
statistical compilation and empirically founded analysis
credited to his influence may have occurred because of the
pressure of other events—the Great Depression, World
War II, and the problems that the years after the war
posed. But this does not concern me greatly; the influence
of any man is joint with a variety of objective circumstances and is felt only if the existing conditions reinforce
it. The joint character of the results is no ground for deny-
ing the importance of a major scholar's contribution.

I am more concerned lest the emphasis on the positive
influence of Mitchell's views and interests mean neglect
of possible negative effects—for example, distortion of
his views because they were misunderstood or improperly
followed by lesser men or because pressure groups may
have utilized them for purposes essentially foreign to
them. The emphasis on empirical observation of economic
behavior may have led to some purely descriptive studies

---

[12] See "Social Science and National Planning" and "Intelligence and the
Guidance of Economic Evolution," in *BASM*, pp. 83–102 and 103–136.

insufficiently illuminated by general hypotheses and yielding results that, at least for a while, proved of little value because they could not be related to a framework that would lend them proper weight and meaning. Insistence on a thorough statistical foundation, influenced by preconceptions reflecting a more timid and less perceptive and objective attitude than Mitchell's to policy action, may have led to advocacy of delay of some action, on the ground that full knowledge was still to be secured, thus making the absence of such knowledge an excuse for inaction, a course overlooking the rather obvious point that inaction (or delay) is also a form of policy, the cost of which may be far greater than the cost of errors that might be committed because the available knowledge is incomplete. I mention these possibilities in recognition of the fact that any meaningful position on the role of economics in relation to policy action is subject to distortion and improper emphasis; and Mitchell's position and views, like those of any major scholar in the difficult field of social studies, were not exempt from such dangers. A thorough evaluation of his contribution would involve a calculus weighing the great positive contributions suggested above against the possible negative effects of the distortions to which his position was prone. But I find it impossible to elaborate such a calculus and see no clear way by which it could be developed to yield sufficiently firm and useful results. I mention it here only to stress that any views that provide guidelines for effective work in a field like economics are liable to distortion and misuse; and that the high value that I assign to the contribution of Mitchell's views and work, while necessarily a strong conviction rather than the product of a cost-return calculus, is not compromised by recognition of some of the low-yield or negative uses to which the position may have occasionally been put.

In conclusion, I would like to raise the issue of whether Mitchell's basic views on the role of economics, much as they have contributed to the extension of tested knowledge, more realistic analysis, and a more open-minded, positive, attitude to policy problems and economic planning, are still valid today and will be in the immediate future. Has their possible value in encouraging greater understanding of economic and social problems, and through it more intelligent decisions on policy questions, been impaired by changes in world conditions and by the shift to the problems which economic study has concentrated upon recently and is likely to emphasize in the near future?

In considering this question, we might note first that, with the mutability of institutions and the rapidity of social change, there are bound to be rapid shifts in the identity of problems that economics is called upon to deal with. The discipline cannot isolate itself from these shifts in identity of the major concerns of the societies within which we live and work; for the changes that bring about these shifts at least contribute new data and intensify search for neglected data that must all be taken into account in reëxamining whatever conclusions have been distilled from past observation and study. And there has been such a shift since Mitchell's lifetime.

It is probably realistic to say that problems of stability, at adequate levels of utilization of resources, and of economic growth (with the connected problems of relations among nations) are the two major groups of problems of concern to current economic study and policy. There is little question that Mitchell's work, and the general approach that guided it, in the field of prices, business cycles, and national income, is of direct use in, and relevance for, problems of economic stability. His insistence on testing empirically the differential responses of various economic groups to short-term stimuli in the course of business cycles; his studies of the behavior of money; his use of national income as the broad quantitative framework within which to observe the changing performance of a country's economy; his critical but constructive attitude towards theories as hypotheses generated within a specific context of some major problems and hence always in need of scrutiny to lay bare the assumptions and to test their validity under changed conditions; his advocacy of usefulness of tested knowledge rather than of preconceived theoretical notions in formulating proper policy actions— all these aspects of his work and approach remain so clearly relevant today to the analysis and solution of problems of economic stability as to obviate need for further discussion.

There may be more of a question when we deal with problems of economic growth, and the closely connected problems of relations among nations. These are in the forefront of economists' concern today, and are likely to be in the near future; but they were certainly not as overwhelming in Mitchell's day, nor as central as were the problems of prices, money, and business cycles in the developed economies of his time. And while Mitchell was interested in secular trends, and presents in Chapter II of his 1927 volume on *Business Cycles* an illuminating discussion that might well be an introductory statement in a book on the growth of the money economies, the present range of problems and policy questions was not the concern of the profession between 1900 and 1940—the years that cover most of Mitchell's active life. Indeed, such problems have not been much discussed in the economic literature since the days of John Stuart Mill and Karl Marx—Schumpeter's 1913 volume being a major exception, although, at that, more a treatise on a secular source of the disturbance of economic equilibrium than a positive theory of economic growth.

If, then, economic theory is to serve these new current problems, it must do so either on the assumption that the patterns of economic behavior established in the study of other, mostly short-term problems (like those of prices and business cycles) can be applied directly, or with easy modifications, to problems of growth, or on the assumption that the generalizations of the classical and Marxian schools, which were concerned with the problems of growth, can still be used. Neither assumption is tenable: short-term analysis generalizations are a treacherous base for inference about long-term changes, particularly economic growth; and the generalizations of the classical and Marxian schools, when tested in terms of the projections drawn from them, have proved to be wrong—one of the reasons why the study of growth problems in accepted economic theory was neglected for the long span of three quarters of a century. We are thus now searching, in haste, for new evidence and new analytical insights. The difficulty is, of course, compounded by the need to bring under observation and analysis a variety of societies, many with institutional structures and patterns different from those of the developed money economies.

It is at this point that the requirement of statistical evidence for adequate economic analysis creates difficulties that should be emphasized. Mitchell properly urged that statistical measures provide the only testable basis for the objective study of mass economic behavior, although he also stressed that quantitative analysis is not possible without an adequate framework of qualitative distinctions. But one other aspect of the reliance on statistical data should also be emphasized. Statistical data are provided largely by society, and only to a very limited extent by scholars themselves. And the supply of such data by a society is largely a function of the stage of its economic development: a pre-industrial, underdeveloped society has greater difficulty in generating quantitative data about its activity and fewer resources to devote to this task than a developed economy, with its literate and quantity-minded population, with its numerous public and private organized units (such as governments or private corporations) geared to proper accounting. We are thus confronted today with the typical situation in which the urgent need for data as a basis for public policies in the less developed countries cannot be met easily, while there is a much greater supply of data, and of intellectual resources to handle them, in the developed countries. Too great an insistence on a fully adequate statistical basis would mean too great a bias in the institutions to be studied, too great an emphasis on the developed countries and too great a neglect of the rest of the world.

Mitchell, I am sure, would have recognized the point quickly. But it is worth stressing explicitly here, for there is today, and there has been for a long time, an over-concentration of economic study on the developed countries, indeed on the country of which an individual student is a native. The very emphasis on statistical thoroughness may have led to concentration on one's own country, where the data are most accessible and most readily understood. But the time has come for us to recognize this bias and attempt a remedy. To put it somewhat differently, the emphasis on the statistical approach led Mitchell to help found and to spend a quarter of a century guiding the destinies of a *national* bureau of economic research. May one suggest that the young Mitchell of today might well found and guide an *international* bureau for comparative study and that, while still urging the advantages of the statistical approach, he would today caution against the temptation to elaborate the details of the well known at the expense of less reliable but indispensable approximations to the less known? In such an extension of statistical measures to other countries and other times, with different institutions and different qualitative distinctions, the very concepts might undergo a change to provide a better reflection of diverse reality than one based on the more traditional concepts geared to a developed money economy. Thus, not only the scope but also the preconceptions of statistical measurement would be subject to an extension and strain not sufficiently emphasized in Mitchell's discussion, which assumed an easy superiority of statistical measurement over other types of empirical data.

Just as too narrow an emphasis on the statistical approach might lead to a national and institutional bias in coverage, and just as insistence on elaborate mathematical tools might result in the selection of problems that can be handled by them and the neglect of more important problems that are not susceptible to such treatment, so there may be a corresponding bias in the use of economic intelligence for policy. We may agree fully with Mitchell that an increase in the stock of tested knowledge is a positive contribution to a more intelligent handling and, all other conditions being equal, solution of policy problems. If so, it is all the more important to try to guide the accretion of tested knowledge in some reasonable relation to the policy weight of the aspects so covered. In this framework, we may be confronted with a choice in which the adequacy of the statistical and empirical data may not be the most important consideration. Obviously, the past neglect in economic study of the economic processes in the less developed countries results in a bias in the supply of data and in the analysis for policy problems: both are far more plentiful for the solution of internal problems of the developed economies than for the intelligent consideration of policies that depend for their success upon the understanding of the economic and social processes in the underdeveloped countries. With all the limitations, there is far less wrong with the way the developed countries, at least within the orbit of the free market economies, solve their domestic problems—for which data are adequate and of which their understanding is not insufficient—than with policies intended to promote what would be, in the long run, optimal relations with the underdeveloped parts of the world. And part of the difficulty lies in the insufficiency of our tested knowledge and hence of our understanding of this large group within the concert of nations.

This bears directly upon the hope for a comprehensive theory of economic behavior. There is little question that the work of Mitchell and his followers contributed greatly to a better—because more comprehensive—theory of the behavior of developed money economies; and the variety of reformulations that occurred confirm Mitchell's hope. But if we, under the pressure of present-day problems, extend the scope of the comprehensive theory of economic behavior to cover its many variants in order to fit the diverse economic growth experience in the immediate past and the proximate future, it becomes clear that we are as far away from such a theory today as we were in Mitchell's lifetime; or at any rate still so far away from it that any progress we may have made seems minor. And in view of the time and difficulties involved in a proper mobilization of testable evidence for such a comprehensive theory, one may ask whether the time scale of expectations —for an adequate theory of economic growth, which may perforce draw upon the other social science disciplines— is much longer than Mitchell had in mind. And if it is, because of the pressure of current problems there may be considerable value even in oversimplified theoretical models. They would at least help to guide one's thinking on pressing questions, utilizing whatever little knowledge is already available, while awaiting the necessarily slow accumulation of comparative statistics and institutional knowledge relating to the diverse parts of the world.

In short, given the mutability of economic and social institutions, which Mitchell emphasized, and the resulting changes in the nature of major economic policy problems, there is a greater conflict today between the requirement that a comprehensive theory of economic behavior be based in large part on the statistical approach and the claim that such a theory will be available for guidance in the solution of policy problems. In the nature of the case, a really comprehensive and statistically founded theory cannot be available until long after any given set of major problems has emerged and been somehow resolved; and it would have been solved, if it was, with the help of the empirical evidence (necessarily partial) available at the time and with a variety of incomplete, partial hypotheses (many claiming more generality than they in fact possess) entertained while the evidence for testing them is still to be assembled. If one assumes, as Mitchell did and as most of us do, that it is next to impossible for economic scholars to ignore the major problems of the day, and if the complete, statistically based theory is something that one strives for but never attains, perhaps one should, in the service of policy problems, admit the necessary limitations of the statistical approach and assign a greater role to incomplete and partial theories that provide reasonable shortcuts. To be sure, they are shortcuts. Their cumulative contribution to economic science may be far more negligible than that of the accumulation of statistical measures and tested generalized patterns of behavior linked by partial hypotheses. But they may be indispensable not only as the best solutions to changing policy problems but also as valuable leads to the qualitative distinctions that are so basic even in statistical measurement and empirical study.

Yet the comments above suggest only a shift in emphasis, somewhat less optimism than Mitchell appeared to entertain concerning the promise of the quantitative approach and the feasibility of a comprehensive theory of economic behavior, and correspondingly more relevance in the shortcut, simplifying, and partial theories. They do not affect the core of Mitchell's position on the roles and relationships of theory, empirical analysis, and policy. Indeed, aside from the qualifications suggested above, which necessarily have an element of personal judgment in them, the greater emphasis in current work on problems of economic growth and relations among nations has served to enhance the value of Mitchell's basic position. The necessary extension of both historical and spatial perspectives, an increased variety of institutional types under observation, and concern for problems that depart considerably from the logic of the market and money economy make Mitchell's counsels all the more appropriate guides. His views on the narrow institutional basis of much economic theorizing and of the influence on it of quick adaptation to pressing current problems should put us in a properly critical frame of mind in examining a "theory" in which economic growth is deduced from simple relations of capital to output or Cobb-Douglas production functions, or one in which a claim for successive stages of development is based either on merely terminological devices or on a few inadequately studied cases. His emphasis on institutions, with their diversity and mutability, is surely relevant today when many problems that economists wrestle with relate to a world in which a relatively uniform complex of production practices (itself changing over time with the dynamics of technological change) is spreading to an increasing number of areas that differ markedly in their historical heritage and in their institutional framework. The statistical measurement that he advocated is just as necessary for the study of economic growth, essentially a quantitative process, and of international relations, in which magnitudes are important, as it was in the study of short-term responses in business cycles. And the extension of the statistical approach that he urged is particularly appropriate today, as a basis not only for proper study of the patterns of economic growth and of international relations, but also for many growth and foreign policy actions. His open-minded attitude to public policy and insistence on the greater use of economic intelligence as its basis is all the more appropriate today, when the problems are so much more complex and the pressure for their adequate consideration makes the play of doctrine or passion so much more dangerous. Whatever we may say of the continued relevance of Mitchell's empirical work—and like all good empirical work, it is absorbed and overlaid by further study so that in and of itself it has played its part—Mitchell's views on the relation between theory, data, and policy in economics appear just as valid and valuable for the progress of our knowledge and policy today as they were when he presented them more than thirty years ago.

FIVE

Institutional Elements in Contemporary Economics

No two writers are likely to define institutional economics in precisely the same way.[1] More than one economist has commented, sometimes with exasperation, on the vagueness of what Schumpeter referred to as "that elusive concept."[2] Paul Homan once declared that "an institutional economics, differentiated from other economics by discoverable criteria, is largely an intellectual fiction, substantially devoid of content."[3]

Obviously, anyone who attempts to offer a precise characterization of institutional economics does so at his own peril. Yet it is essential that we make clear what it is we are talking about. Hence I shall try to set down a list of characteristics which I associate with the term, recognizing full well that the elements I have chosen to emphasize

---

[1] I should like to take this opportunity to thank Mr. Gunter Wittich for his help in the preparation of this paper.

[2] In his essay on Mitchell in *Ten Great Economists from Marx to Keynes* (New York: Oxford University Press, 1951), p. 243.

[3] "An Appraisal of Institutional Economics," *American Economic Review*, XXII (March, 1932), 15.

may not be precisely those to which other (and more informed) students would give primary weight.

Joseph Dorfman has stated that institutional economics
had a common base in its "criticism of traditional economic theory and its presumptions concerning human
motivations and the universality of capitalist institutional
factors," and that the "institutionalists had the feeling that
traditional economics did not provide effective tools for
understanding and dealing with a developing economy
and the problems left by the war [of 1914–18]. They also
objected to the inadequate practical recognition given to
history, statistics, and such newer group phenomena as
trade unions, corporations, and trade associations. They
sought not only to broaden the range of economic theory,
but also to relate it to the contributions of the other social
disciplines." [4]

I shall take the risk of going a bit further than Professor
Dorfman does. The term "institutional economics" sug-
gests to me a series of propositions, which, taken together,
add up to a particular way of approaching the study of
economics. [5]

(1) Economic behavior is strongly conditioned by the institutional environment (in all its manifestations) within which
economic activity takes place, and economic behavior in turn
affects the institutional environment.

(2) This process of mutual interaction is an evolutionary
one. The environment changes, and, as it does, so do the

---

[4] *The Economic Mind in American Civilization,* Vol. IV (New York:
Viking Press, 1959), pp. 352–353. Note also Professor Dorfman's comment,
in his essay in the present volume, that institutionalism "is not economics
in the usual sense, but a slice of the whole development of civilization in
the United States since the end of the Civil War."

[5] A number of these characteristics may also suggest Marxian economics
to the reader. This would not be surprising, because there is more than a
passing resemblance between American institutionalism and Marxian
economics. This is a matter to which we shall return, in a somewhat indirect way, in the last section of this paper.

determinants of economic behavior. Hence the need for an "evolutionary approach" to economics.

(3) In this evolutionary process of interaction, a key role is played by the (largely conflicting) conditions imposed by modern technology and by the pecuniary institutions of modern capitalism.

(4) Economics is more concerned with conflict than with a harmonious order in which unconscious coöperation results from the free play of market forces.

(5) Since conflict underlies so many economic relationships, and since these relationships are not immutable, there is room and need for social control of economic activity.

(6) We need to learn all that we can from psychology, sociology, anthropology, and law if we are to understand why human beings act as they do in their economic roles. People are not maximizing automata reacting mechanically in an institutional vacuum.

(7) Granted the preceding assumptions, much of orthodox economic theory is either wrong or irrelevant because it makes demonstrably false assumptions and does not ask the really important questions. A new, broader, evolutionary theory— based on behavioral assumptions derived from the other social sciences and on detailed knowledge of the evolution and present characteristics of the institutional environment—needs to be constructed. A wide variety of empirical studies must precede the attempt to construct such a broader, evolutionary, and more realistic corpus of theory.

It is obvious that not all writers classed as institutionalists would emphasize the same elements in this list. Commons and Mitchell were much less antagonistic to orthodox theory than was Veblen. The advocacy of measures of social control was strongest in Commons and in Veblen's followers and least strong in Veblen himself.[6]

---

[6] Veblen became much more an avowed advocate of social change after World War I than he had been before; but his proposals were usually

Empirical research meant different things to each of these men; of the three, only Mitchell made significant contributions in the area of applied quantitative economics. The evolutionary approach shows up most strongly, of course, in Veblen. The emphasis on conflict is most explicit in Commons; it appears but in a quite different form in Veblen; it plays hardly any role in Mitchell's work.[7] When we look at their avowed disciples, the differences multiply. Many had little in common beyond an antitheoretical bias, a propensity for detailed empirical work, and a strong desire for social and economic reform.[8]

To what extent are the characteristics I have listed—the "institutional elements" in the title of this paper—reflected in the main body of contemporary economics? The answer is a very mixed one, indeed. Most of my "institutional" characteristics can be found in the economic literature of the last twenty years, and it can be fairly said that Veblen, Commons, Mitchell, and their disciples have left a lasting impression on economics—on the questions

quite drastic, calling for a substantial reordering of society, and he had little use for the kinds of ameliorative reform that were so enthusiastically pushed by many of his and Commons' followers—and a good deal of which came to be embodied in legislation under the New Deal. Compare, for example, A. G. Gruchy, "The Concept of National Planning in Institutional Economics," *Southern Economic Journal*, VI (October, 1939), 121–144; also, David Riesman, *Thorstein Veblen, a Critical Interpretation* (New York: Scribner, 1953), Chs. 5–6. As for Commons, "he more than any other economist was responsible for the conversion into public policy of reform proposals designed to alleviate the defects in the industrial system." Dorfman, *op. cit.*, Vol. IV, p. 377.

[7] For some of the differences between Veblen and Mitchell in this respect, see A. L. Harris, "Types of Institutionalism," *Journal of Political Economy*, XL (December, 1932), 721–749. On the roles of conflict and "collective action" in Commons' writings, see Professor Chamberlain's essay in this volume.

[8] See, for example, the article by Homan previously cited; also the comments by J. S. Gambs on the "neo-Veblenians" in *Beyond Supply and Demand* (New York: Columbia University Press, 1946).

economists ask and on the manner in which they go about answering them.[9]

While this is true, I think it can also be said that, in many respects, orthodox economic theory is about as vulnerable today to Veblen's barbs as when he first hurled them more than 60 years ago.[10] Veblen would still find reason to say of much of today's economics, as he did of economics around the turn of the century, that it results in "a body of logically consistent propositions concerning the normal relations of things—a system of economic taxonomy. At its worst, it is a body of maxims for the conduct of business and a polemical discussion of disputed points of policy." [11] This was a harsh judgment when it was published in 1898 (how harsh depends, as is usually the case with Veblen, on how literally one interprets him), and it would be equally harsh today. But much of what bothered Veblen then would certainly bother him now if he were alive to read the current literature. Indeed, he might be moved to find some new pejorative adjectives to cast at the current generation of economists.

Let us consider a few examples of the kinds of contrast

---

[9] Richard Ruggles stated in 1952 that: "In the last twenty years the spirit of the institutionalists has permeated the whole of economic analysis and has become more or less integrated with the other approaches. The revolutionary fervor is gone, yet in many fields of economics the imprint of institutionalism remains." In B. F. Haley, ed., *Survey of Contemporary Economics*, Vol. II (Homewood, Ill.: Irwin, 1952), p. 427. See also Kenneth Boulding's comment that "the indirect influence of institutionalism has been very great." "A New Look at Institutionalism," *American Economic Review: Papers and Proceedings*, XLVII (May, 1957), 12.

[10] Let me record one important exception here. What Veblen called the "animism" of classical economics has largely disappeared. (Indeed, Veblen even remarked on its gradual attenuation.) Formal economics is today much more impersonal and objective and more free of teleological propensities than was the classical economics that Veblen criticized.

[11] "Why Is Economics Not an Evolutionary Science?" reprinted in *The Place of Science in Modern Civilisation* (New York: Huebsch, 1919), pp. 67–68.

contemporary economics offers to one who looks for the institutional elements that I listed earlier. The strong mathematical trend in economic theorizing tends to encourage neglect of the institutional determinants of economic behavior. At the same time, the great expansion of interest in problems of economic development has led to a new emphasis on the influence of the institutional environment on economic relationships. Or, to cite another contrast, the elaboration of formal theory, much of it in nonoperational terms, has gone hand in hand with a tremendous enrichment of statistical data and a proliferation of useful empirical work. Or again, much of neo-Keynesian growth and cycle theory, with its almost exclusive concern with the interrelationships among a few aggregative real variables, not only neglects the institutional factors that influence economic change but seems to be concerned with a nonexistent world in which there are no prices and no money. Yet, in the same journals in which these simplified models are presented, we can find valuable studies of stabilization policy, the newer type of quantitative historical studies, or articles dealing with the bearing of the emergence of new types of financial institutions on monetary theory and policy.

The economics that Veblen and his followers attacked was orthodox static theory, with its assumptions of maximizing behavior within a fixed set of pecuniary institutions, and with a minimum of interest in either empirical verification or in the study of how institutional determinants of economic behavior had evolved or might be changed through private or public action. But a great deal of water has gone under the bridge since the early years of the century, in economics as well as in other branches of knowledge. While static allocation theory still plays a central role in economic analysis, what economists write about and the tools they use have changed radically in the last 60 years. Let us see to what extent various of these changes have tended to make economics more or less institutional in the sense in which we are using the word.

The most striking change has undoubtedly been the development of aggregative economics. On the theoretical side, this includes static employment theory, business-cycle theory, and the beginnings of a theory of growth. It also includes national income accounting and the host of empirical studies that seek to make use of the wealth of data in the national income accounts. It includes major contributions to stabilization policy, on the monetary and particularly on the fiscal side. We should note also the newer literature on inflation, with its implications regarding the effect of institutional relationships on the size of labor's share in the national income and on the consequent behavior of the level of wages and prices.

I am not surprised that Professor Ayres, in his paper in this series, comments approvingly on the "national income approach to the study of the economy," although I must confess that I do not understand why it "is in a quite literal sense Veblenian" or why "macro-economics is Veblenian economics." As I have already suggested and shall suggest again later, it can even be argued that the development of a quantitatively oriented macro-economics centering on simple, unchanging relationships among a few aggregative variables expressed in real terms is quite alien to the institutionalist, and particularly to Veblen's, approach to economics. It is also alien to the spirit of Mitchell's work and to that of his disciples in the National Bureau of Economic Research.

A second major change in economics is associated with the upsurge of interest in problems of economic development, particularly in the so-called backward countries. Here economics has truly "gone institutional." It is in this area, more than any other, that we find systematic work being done on the way in which the institutional environment, in all its various dimensions, impinges on economic behavior and on the way in which customs and habits inherited from the past conflict with the requirements of modern technology. By their very nature, problems of economic development are dynamic and evolutionary. Here, more than in most branches of economics, interdisciplinary research is necessary.[12] And the normative emphasis stands out—how to make "the critical minimum effort" or to create the conditions necessary for a "take-off" so that a cumulative, self-sustaining growth in output per capita becomes possible.

I should add that what we loosely call the field of economic development or growth falls broadly into two areas: (1) the particular study of backward or under-developed countries and (2) the general study of the determinants of growth, including the attempt to explain differences in growth rates among various countries (the economically advanced as well as the underdeveloped) and during different periods of time. The comments in the preceding paragraph apply particularly to the first area, but they also have some application to the second— as illustrated, for example, by the work of Simon Kuznets and by the debates on the reasons for the recent slow growth of the American economy. There is little of an institutional character, however, in the formal models that make up a good deal of the recent literature on the theory of growth.

In another area, we find that study of the behavior of the firm has been greatly extended. New avenues of investiga-

---

[12] "The economics of growth is, therefore, the field of work in which the dependence of economics on its sister social sciences appears in a supreme degree." Moses Abramovitz, "Economics of Growth," in *Survey of Contemporary Economics,* Vol. II, p. 177.

tion have been opened up at the same time that economists have lost their earlier confidence in the usefulness of
a simple model that derives the conditions of profits maximization from conventional cost and revenue functions.
The theory of the firm has been enriched, and also complicated, by what is called organization theory, which in
turn has borrowed from sociology, psychology, statistical
theory, and other disciplines.[13] The assumption of profits
maximization has been challenged by a number of
writers. Notions of strategy and conflict have been introduced through game theory, as well as by elaboration of
orthodox oligopoly theory.[14] Attention has been paid to
the kinds of information available to the decision maker
and to the costs of obtaining such information. The effect
of the external environment and of internal institutional
arrangements on decision making within the firm has
been explored by various writers, with the result, already
noted, that we have lost some of our earlier confidence
that profit maximization is the only decision rule needed
in the study of the behavior of the individual firm. These
various developments, however, have not yet been fully
integrated into a general, and generally accepted, "organizational" theory of the firm.[15]

A more important development has been the recogni-

---

[13] Cf. H. A. Simon, "Theories of Decision-Making in Economics and Behavioral Science," *American Economic Review*, XLIX (June, 1959),
253–283. For a review of the literature on organization theory, see
J. G. March and H. A. Simon, *Organizations* (New York: Wiley, 1958).

[14] Note Professor Chamberlain's comment (p. 94, above) that "those
economists who are working with simulation techniques, bargaining
relationships, game theory, and the like, are probably more nearly in the
Commons tradition. They too are likely to find difficulty in fitting their
developing concepts into a viable theoretical system."

[15] On all this, see A. G. Papandreou, "Some Basic Problems in the Theory
of the Firm," in *Survey of Contemporary Economics*, Vol. II. As Papandreou observes (*ibid.*, p. 183), economics has not yet "evolved a theory of
conscious cooperation."

tion that departures from perfect competition are the rule
rather than the exception. The work of Chamberlin and
Mrs. Robinson led to a revolution in price theory and to
the development of new analytical tools to apply to the
study of industrial markets. This is an area in which advances in economics have had an important effect on legal
developments. Law and economics continue to interact as,
in a sense, they always have; but, somewhat reversing the
direction of influence that played such an important role
in Commons's thinking, judicial interpretation has been
affected to a significant degree by the new concepts and
analytical tools developed by economists. Edward Mason
has said that "The theory of oligopoly has been aptly described as a ticket of admission to institutional economics," [16] and perhaps the same may be said of the theory of
monopolistic competition generally. But, if price theory
has to some extent become institutional, it can also be said
that empirical studies of industrial markets have become
much more analytical.

Labor economics has long been a favorite hunting
ground of economists who considered themselves institutionalists. This circumstance is partly due to the influence
of Commons. Today, there is very little labor economics
that is not, in one way or another, institutional in its
orientation. This is true even of those labor economists
who do not think of themselves as being particularly in the
tradition. Trade unions, powerful employers and employer associations, the network of labor law, and the
process of collective bargaining create an institutional
environment that no student of wage determination or of
the labor movement can neglect. Classical wage theory has
largely gone by the board, and we have not yet come up
with anything to take its place. Due attention to the in-

---

[16] Quoted by Bernard Haley, in H. S. Ellis, ed., *A Survey of Contemporary
Economics,* Vol. I (Philadelphia: Blakiston, 1948) , p. 17.

stitutional environment has its rewards for the economist in the greater realism of his analysis and in the increased relevance of his findings for public policy. But a price must also be paid in terms of greater fuzziness in his theoretical analysis and perhaps of restricted opportunity for sweeping generalizations.[17] Thus far, in the evolution of labor economics, the gain has outweighed the cost.

It should be added that, while we no longer have an accepted body of wage theory that has much explanatory value in labor markets characterized by collective bargaining, labor economics—particularly that concerned with the level and structure of wages—has taken on an analytical orientation that leaves some old-fashioned institutionalists unhappy. Work being done today on wage differentials, on labor's share, on the relation between wages and prices, and so on involves the use of theoretical and empirical tools that are not needed in historical studies of particular unions or in essays on the theory of the labor movement.[18]

Another striking change in economics has been the trend toward quantification, a trend which Mitchell in particular anticipated eagerly. This is a trend of which those with institutionalist leanings would presumably approve, but,

---

[17] But while the opportunity for generalizations about wage determination may be restricted, new opportunities for generalization in other directions become possible—regarding the evolution of labor-management relations, industrialization and development of an industrial labor force, the structure and functioning of trade unions, etc. An increasing amount of work on the institutional aspects of the trade union and the employer-worker relationship is being done in the social sciences other than economics. Cf. W. Galenson and S. M. Lipset, eds., *Labor and Trade Unionism* (New York: Wiley, 1960), pp. v–vi.

[18] Speaking of the labor field, Lloyd Reynolds commented shortly after the war that: "It is probably more true today than it was a generation ago that the people most highly trained in deductive analysis are among those best informed on factual questions and most active in empirical investigation." *A Survey of Contemporary Economics*, Vol. I, p. 287. This trend toward the blending of theory and practice has continued.

as I shall indicate shortly, systematic quantification tends to carry economics away from the kind of institutional approach that Veblen or Commons, or for that matter Mitchell, would have advocated.

This tendency is most readily seen in the current predilection for reformulating economic theory in mathematical terms. The gains from doing so are obvious, although sometimes a substantial sacrifice is also involved. Mathematics is virtually essential for the rigorous handling of complicated relationships. In general, however, mathematical treatment tends to depersonalize and "deinstitutionalize" economic theory.[19] Mathematical models tend, on the whole, to lead to a mechanistic view of the economy, to interest in stable relationships among (at least conceptually) quantifiable magnitudes; the volitional role of the economic actors is minimized; there is little or no consideration of institutional constraints and of how and why these constraints change over time. This is true even of what we call dynamic theory, as represented, for example, by the growth and cycle models that dot the postwar literature.

Mathematics is useful not merely in the formulation of theory. It has also come to play an essential twofold role in the process of verification, of hypothesis testing. First of all, mathematics helps to put theory in a form suitable for testing. And, second, it contributes powerfully to the development of tools with whose help such testing can be done. There could be no econometrics without mathematics, and without mathematics we should not have had the newer developments in sampling theory and in statistical inference generally.

In any event, there has been this marked trend toward quantification. We have more theory that is expressed in

---

[19] This may not be true of some of the mathematical treatment in organization and decision theory.

a quantitative form suitable for testing;[20] there is an enormous body of data available for use;[21] our statistical tools have been greatly improved; and computers of frightening efficiency are at hand to help us. Institutionally oriented economists have participated in these developments, but only up to a point. When it comes to the formal testing of hypotheses and the development of new econometric techniques, the main work is being done by those who are pretty much in the orthodox tradition, and particularly by the younger generation with the requisite training in mathematics and statistics. I have already suggested why this sort of work is not likely to appeal to the institutionalist.[22]

One could go on almost indefinitely listing ways in which the content of economics and the interests of economists have changed in the last couple of generations. Let me end my own enumeration by merely mentioning a few more of these changes: a new interest in population growth occasioned by the so-called population explosion; new developments in the theory of economic planning at both the micro and macro levels; the beginning of an

---

[20] This is a development that Mitchell predicted. But he was wrong in also predicting that the trend toward quantification would lead economic theory to put more emphasis on the importance of institutions. See the quotation from "Quantitative Analysis in Economic Theory" cited by Professor Kuznets, p. 99, above.

[21] As Professor Kuznets points out, this is a development for which Mitchell and his followers (including Kuznets himself) are in good part responsible.

[22] These comments require a footnote on two different trends which are observable in recent quantitative studies. One is illustrated by the work of the National Bureau of Economic Research, which is in the tradition established by Mitchell. Here the emphasis is on systematic observation with a minimum of *a priori* theorizing—what Koopmans once referred to as "Measurement without Theory." In contrast is the econometric type of work, which sets out to test an explicit, mathematically formulated set of hypotheses. There is, of course, a considerable body of empirical work which, in the use it makes of theory, falls in an intermediate position. An example is the newer work in quantitative economic history.

interest in the economics of education; an awakening to the need for systematic work on urban and regional development; a new analytical interest in problems of social legislation (medical care, old-age and unemployment insurance, education, and so on) ; and concern with the economic aspects of the accelerating advance in science and technology. For the most part, these are developments of which an earlier generation of institutionalists would have approved.

It is clear, as I suggested earlier, that what passes for orthodox economics is today more institutional than it was before, say, the Great Depression. In varying degrees, and more so in some fields than in others, contemporary economics has at least partially absorbed the institutional elements I listed earlier.

In an important sense, however, the central core of economic theory is about as "noninstitutional" as it was in Veblen's day. Samuelson's *Foundations* or Hicks's *Value and Capital* is developed in much more of an institutional vacuum than was Marshall's *Principles*.[23] Theoretically inclined economists, with some exceptions, do not take kindly to the study of institutional arrangements or institutional development. Despite some of the new developments in the theory of the firm and of market behavior, micro theory is still concerned primarily with the kind of "equilibrium economics" which Veblen so severely

---

[23] This is true even if we accept Mitchell's dictum that Marshall had "no adequate appreciation of the intimacy with which pecuniary concepts have entered into the minds of men and formed their habits of thinking." "The Rationality of Economic Activity: II," *Journal of Political Economy*, XVIII (March, 1910) , 207. Yet Veblen spoke not unsympathetically of (somewhat embryonic) evolutionary tendencies that he discerned in Marshall's work. "The Preconceptions of Economic Science: III," in *The Place of Science in Modern Civilisation*, p. 175.

criticized.[24] (This is even more true if we include the considerable literature on "stability conditions," the pure theory of economic welfare, and related matters.) The main body of professional opinion holds that this kind of economics raises significant questions and results in analytical tools that do help us to understand how, in important respects, the economy (at least, our kind of economy) functions. The same view is held even more widely regarding the usefulness of macro-economic theory, even in its more abstract formulations.

The same conventional wisdom, to use Galbraith's deliberately provocative term, does not deny that orthodox economics has failed to give us a general and dynamic theory of social behavior. Most economists would argue that this is not the purpose of economic analysis. No one would deny the need to study how social and legal, as well as economic, institutions have evolved and how this evolution has affected economic behavior. But this is an area which most economists are inclined to leave to sociologists, historians, and anthropologists. The main trend in economics has been irresistibly toward analytical rigor and toward quantification. Physics—not anthropology or even biology—is the science economics has chosen most to emulate.[25] Where, as in the theory of economic development, economic theorists (and I am talking here only about the theorists) have had to deal explicitly with institutional factors, they have typically started with a quantifiable variable (total output or output per capita) and have sought to relate this to other conventional vari-

---

[24] But without the "natural law" overtones or reliance on a hedonistic psychology that Veblen, Mitchell, and others criticized.

[25] There are, of course, a number of exceptions to this generalization among economic theorists who have left their mark on the profession. I would mention particularly Schumpeter, with his essentially "organic" theory of economic development.

ables (like capital formation). So far as possible, they
have dealt with institutional factors as constraints which
are possibly subject to discrete changes through collective
action.

Thus we arrive at the "mixed picture" to which I referred earlier. Let me summarize in the following way.
The central core of theory and the tool building that has
gone on in such theoretical analysis have not been much
affected by our institutional elements. Veblen's primary
aim, it has been said, "was the destruction of orthodox
economics." [26] In this aim, obviously, neither he nor his
followers succeeded. Yet in many branches of theory—
and particularly where theory seeks to relate directly to
the real world—economic analysis has become more institutional. And in applied work, economics is at one and
the same time both more institutional and more rigorously analytical than it was a generation or two ago.

In this concluding section, let me revert to the last of the
propositions that I used to define the institutionalist approach. This involved both a negative and an affirmative
statement. On the negative side, the argument runs, orthodox theory makes demonstrably false assumptions and fails
to ask the really important questions. Affirmatively, we
need a new, broad, and evolutionary type of economic
theory based on a detailed understanding of the evolution
and characteristics of the institutional environment within
which economic activity goes on. In Veblen's words, we
need a theory of "the process of cumulative change . . .
in the methods of dealing with the material means of
life," [27] or, as Mitchell put it, a comprehensive theory of

---

[26] Max Lerner, in *The Portable Veblen* (New York: Viking Press, 1958),
p. 30.

[27] "Why Is Economics Not an Evolutionary Science?" *op. cit.*, pp. 70–71.

economic behavior that takes the cumulative change of institutions as its chief concern.[28]

We know that the institutionalists themselves did not develop such a comprehensive and evolutionary theory. What can we say about efforts in this direction in contemporary economics? Is orthodox economics asking the "really important questions" and is it seeking to answer these questions within a sufficiently comprehensive and evolutionary context?

In one sense, of course, orthodox economic theory has long had a grand design represented by the general theory of static equilibrium. The classical writers, in addition, had the elements of a dynamic system—what William Baumol has referred to as the "magnificent dynamics" of the classical school—although this system was confined within a straitjacket imposed by too sweeping an application of Malthusian population theory, a questionable psychology, an insufficient appreciation of the importance of technological change, the assumption of a fixed set of social and economic institutions, and undue preoccupation with the law of diminishing returns. In recent years, we have begun to take the long view again, and a new start has been made on a theory of growth.

Nonetheless, I think it is fair to say that orthodox theory does lack a grand design, an overall view that takes due account of both time and space and also concerns itself with the cumulative interaction of economic behavior and the changing institutional environment. With the tools they now use, economists have little to say about where we are going, and why, or about the dynamic interaction, in the long run, of economic, political, and social institutions. These are among the "fundamental questions which

---

[28] Cf. "The Prospects of Economics," in R. G. Tugwell, ed., *The Trend of Economics* (New York: Knopf, 1924) , pp. 24, 27.

make us all uneasy" to which Professor Chamberlain referred at the end of his paper on Commons.

Is it unfair to suggest that most of contemporary economic analysis is fragmentary, concerned largely with refining our understanding of things as they are (or as they would be given the assumptions we make), too lacking in historical perspective, and formulated in at least a partial sociological, psychological, and political vacuum? It has been said that "the institutionalized social sciences . . . are shying away from the risky ventures of general interpretations of human events." [29] On the whole, this is true also of contemporary economics. Economists have acquired a degree of technical skill far beyond anything possessed by their predecessors of a generation or two ago, but it is chiefly the skill of the technician. Let it not be thought that I disparage the importance of this work. Whether in exploring the mathematics of static equilibrium theory, or testing dynamic econometric models, or studying the effects of the Common Market, or doing the essential staff work in one government department or another, the economist's technical skills have contributed both to the sum of human knowledge and to modern man's ability to have some influence on his environment. But most of this work is done within the framework of the particular institutions prevailing in the Western world in the middle of the twentieth century. Some exception, of course, must be made for the considerable effort that is going into the study of the underdeveloped parts of the world, but even here the work has, I think, been strongly conditioned by the use of analytical tools and viewpoints reflecting the attitudes and preconceptions of Western economic orthodoxy.

In the sense of asking the really big questions about the

---

[29] S. M. Lipset and Leo Lowenthal, eds., *Culture and Social Character* (Glencoe, Ill.: The Free Press, 1961), p. v.

economic aspects of society—which, because they are big, must be concerned with the changing institutional fabric of society—contemporary economics is not as institutional as it might be, although it might be said that contemporary Western economists are prepared to be more institutional in dealing with other parts of the world than they are in studying the particular societies in which they live and do most of their work. One can, of course, think of various exceptions to this perhaps too sweeping generalization. I hasten to mention one who has just preceded me in this series. Simon Kuznets has been asking probing questions regarding the nature of and the reasons for the different patterns and rates of economic development in different countries, and his work over the years in measuring the growth of output and capital formation has resulted in the construction of a substantial foundation of quantitative knowledge in an area that was once littered with speculation and ignorance. I am sure, however, that he would be first to say that a comprehensive and comparative theory of growth is still far in the future.

I might mention one other writer who, while he has not constructed a broad and evolutionary theory of economic behavior, shows a striking propensity to ask big and uncomfortable questions. This is J. K. Galbraith. The questions asked in *The Affluent Society* are big and disturbing questions; they have to do with the changing interaction between economic behavior and important aspects of the institutional environment; [30] and, in its mocking of the "conventional wisdom" of economics, the book is clearly in the institutionalist tradition.

If we put these and other partial exceptions aside, it seems to me that so far in this century we have had only one reasonably close approximation to a comprehensive and evolutionary theory which, at the same time that it

---

[30] This can also be said of his earlier analysis of "countervailing power."

incorporates the standard economic variables and deals with many of the usual economic relationships, also presents a theory of cumulative change in terms of the interaction between economic behavior and the evolving institutional environment. This institutional economist did not come out of the American Midwest but out of Central Europe; his general outlook could hardly have been more different from that of Veblen or Commons; his personal tastes were for nineteenth century liberalism and the culture of the Old World at the same time that his logic led him to predict the demise of capitalist institutions. I am speaking of course of Joseph Schumpeter.

If we take Schumpeter's major writings and measure his institutionalism against the criteria I listed earlier, we find that:

(1) He clearly placed great weight on the interaction between economic behavior and the institutional environment. He repeatedly stressed "that 'economic laws' are much less stable than are the 'laws' of any physical science, that they work out differently in different institutional conditions, and that neglect of this fact has been responsible for many an aberration." [31] Thus his concern with the changing conditions under which the entrepreneur practices his innovating role, his institutionalist approach to the theory of interest, his treatment of competition and monopoly in the light of the conditions created by technological change, or his analysis of the way in which the capitalist process undermines its own institutional framework.[32]

(2) It hardly needs to be said again that Schumpeter had an evolutionary approach to economics. "The essen-

---

[31] *History of Economic Analysis* (New York: Oxford University Press, 1954), p. 34.

[32] Cf. Haberler's essay on Schumpeter in *Quarterly Journal of Economics*, LXIV (August, 1950), 363 ff.

tial point to grasp," he said, "is that in dealing with capitalism we are dealing with an evolutionary process." [33] This approach was already to be found in 1911 in *The Theory of Economic Development;* the same evolutionary emphasis, but broadened to include the study of the institutional changes that he thought would bring about the end of capitalism, is to be found thirty years later in *Capitalism, Socialism, and Democracy.* The subtitle of his two-volume study, *Business Cycles,* is "A Theoretical, Historical, and Statistical Analysis of the Capitalist Process."

(3) As did Veblen, but in a quite different way, Schumpeter emphasized the relations between technology and the institutions of modern capitalism: the rationality underlying both business behavior and modern science, the way technological progress emerges out of capitalist profit seeking (a radically different view from Veblen's), and eventually the routinization of the entrepreneurial function with the "trustification of capitalism." And thus his final conclusion that "Since capitalist enterprise, by its very achievements, tends to automatize progress, . . . it tends to make itself superfluous—to break to pieces under the pressure of its own success." [34]

(4) Unlike some American institutionalists, Schumpeter did not denigrate the role of markets in bringing about unconscious coöperation among the participants in economic activity. He was too much of an economic theorist in the orthodox tradition for that. Yet, as we have already seen, conflict plays a key role in his conception of evolving capitalism: the conflict between the new and the old involved in his notion of "creative destruction" and, more importantly, the "almost universal hostility to its

[33] *Capitalism, Socialism, and Democracy* (2d ed.; New York: Harper, 1947) , p. 82.
[34] *Ibid.,* p. 134.

own social order" which the capitalist process eventually tends to produce.[35] As Professor Haberler has observed, Schumpeter was "closer to Marx than to Walras, Böhm-Bawerk and, even more, than to Keynes." [36]

(5) Schumpeter's views on the need for social control were, of course, radically different from those of writers we usually think of as being institutional economists. He was opposed to most of the New-Deal types of measures that the latter tended to advocate. He felt that many so-called measures of social reform were legislating capitalism out of existence. He lacked the optimism inherent in the American institutionalist tradition; he was a fatalist with a Marxian sort of determinism. "Mankind is not free to choose. . . . Things economic and social move by their own momentum and the ensuing situations compel individuals and groups to behave in certain ways whatever they may wish to do. . . ." [37] (Contrast this with the volitionalism in Commons.) As an economist, he "did not wish to advocate anything." [38] In the preface to *Business Cycles* he was careful to say: "I recommend no policy and propose no plan." [39] Like the earlier Veblen, he tried to look with Olympian detachment on a world which was changing in ways which did not fit his personal tastes.

(6) In his emphasis on the other social sciences, Schumpeter fits our sixth criterion extremely well. *Capitalism, Socialism, and Democracy* belongs to sociology and political science as well as to economics; of the analytical tools available to the economist, he considered economic history the most important; [40] and, in describing the tool-box of the economist, he added what he called "economic

[35] *Ibid.*, p. 143.
[36] *Op. cit.*, pp. 362–363.
[37] *Capitalism, Socialism, and Democracy*, p. 129.
[38] *Ibid.*, p. xi.
[39] *Business Cycles*, Vol. I (New York: McGraw-Hill, 1939), p. vi.
[40] Cf. *History of Economic Analysis*, p. 12.

sociology"—how people "came to behave as they do"—to the standard tools of history, theory, and statistics.[41] Admittedly, the way he used psychology, sociology, and philosophy differed markedly from that of the American institutionalists, with their emphasis on pragmatism and a behavioral psychology.

(7) I have already considered my seventh criterion. To make my point again, Schumpeter, perhaps more than any economist since Marx, did have a broad, evolutionary, and institutionally oriented theory of the functioning of the economy.[42]

I am sure that Schumpeter would have winced at my characterization of him as an institutionalist, and I am fairly confident that those who do consider themselves institutionalists would reject him out of hand. He obviously stands outside the tradition of native American institutionalism. He admired and used classical equilibrium theory (he even referred to himself as a "theoretical *gourmet*") [43]; he clearly showed the influence of Marx in his view of history; he had little of the innate optimism or confidence in the efficacy of social tinkering displayed by most institutionalists.[44] Yet, if we accept my characterization of what constitutes an institutionalist approach to economics, it is hardly possible to exclude him.

If Schumpeter fits most of the institutionalist criteria, why is there likely to be hesitation in putting him alongside the founding fathers of institutional economics? The

---

[41] *Ibid.*, pp. 20–21.

[42] It is worth citing, in this connection, Mitchell's approving comment that "Marx saw the central problem of economics in the cumulative change of economic institutions." "The Prospects of Economics," *op. cit.*, p. 18.

[43] Haberler, *op. cit.*, p. 368.

[44] It has been observed that "Schumpeter was neither a reformer nor an enthusiastic partisan of capitalism, socialism, planning, or any other 'ism' . . ." Haberler, *op. cit.*, p. 371. This was in marked contrast to the reformist tradition that institutionalism developed.

reason is partly that his background was European, and most of us think of institutionalism as very much an American phenomenon. But I think the explanation goes a bit deeper. Schumpeter was an institutionalist in the same sense as was Marx (although, of course, he disagreed with Marx strongly on both economic and political grounds); that is, he took the entire story of capitalist evolution and possible decline as his province. American institutionalists, I think it is fair to say, have not been willing to go this far in their institutionalism. On the whole, they have been concerned more with particular institutions than with the entire institutional framework—and, more often than not, within a limited time perspective and with reference chiefly to American conditions. They have therefore not produced the comprehensive, evolutionary, and institutionally oriented theory that they sought. Their perspective in time and space was more limited than they realized. They deprived themselves of the analytical insights that could have been derived both from classical and neoclassical theory and from Marxian dynamics. They thought very largely in terms of American economic and social conditions during a few decades. And, in a sense, they did not ask big enough questions, did not equip themselves with the tools to answer systematically the questions that they did ask. In short, by the criteria I have suggested, Schumpeter was too much an institutionalist—and also he integrated orthodox theory and his institutionalism too thoroughly—to be regarded as in the tradition of institutional economics.

Contemporary economics does not yet have the tools required for a comprehensive and evolutionary theory of economic behavior that would take appropriate account of the main lines of institutional change. We are more likely to develop these tools if we are more insistent about asking the big and troublesome questions—questions of the sort (but not limited to those) which Schumpeter, more than most of his contemporaries, did ask and attempt to answer. We should not be afraid to keep on asking: how has economic society evolved and where is it going, in this and other countries? This calls not only for an overall theory of socio-economic development but also for detailed studies of particular institutional relationships and of their dynamic interaction with the economic magnitudes with which economists feel most at home. We are making some progress in this latter direction, and it is in this somewhat piecemeal sense that economics is more institutional than it once was.

Selected Bibliographies

These bibliographies are provided for those readers who wish to examine the thought of Veblen, Commons, and Mitchell in the original. The lists have been selected from complete or virtually complete bibliographies available in the following works: Joseph Dorfman, *Thorstein Veblen and His America* (New York: Viking, 1934), pp. 519–524; John R. Commons, *The Economics of Collective Action* (New York: Macmillan, 1950), pp. 377–407; Arthur F. Burns, ed., *Wesley Clair Mitchell, The Economic Scientist* (New York: National Bureau of Economic Research, 1952), pp. 343–366. The authors and publishers of these books have kindly given their consent for this republication.

In general, the bibliographies that follow are of major works, that is, books and articles. The items omitted consist primarily of book reviews. Several of the books of the institutionalists have appeared in paperback, among them Veblen's *Theory of the Leisure Class* and *Theory of Business Enterprise*, Commons' *Institutional Economics* and *Legal Foundations of Capitalism*, and Mitchell's *Business Cycles* (in part). Because of the rapid turnover in the paperback market, these items have not been added to the bibliographies. As in the original sources, the selected bibliographies that follow are arranged chronologically.

SELECTED BIBLIOGRAPHY OF THORSTEIN VEBLEN

1884

"Kant's Critique of Judgment," *Journal of Speculative Philosophy*, July, pp. 260–274.

1891

"Some Neglected Points in the Theory of Socialism," *Annals of the American Academy of Political and Social Science*, Nov., pp. 345–362.

1892

"Böhm-Bawerk's Definition of Capital and the Source of Wages," *Quarterly Journal of Economics*, Jan., pp. 247–252.

" 'The Overproduction Fallacy,' " *Quarterly Journal of Economics*, July, pp. 484–492.

"The Price of Wheat Since 1867," *Journal of Political Economy*, Dec., pp. 68–103 and appendix pp. 156–161.

"The Food Supply and the Price of Wheat," *Journal of Political Economy*, June, pp. 365–379.

1894

"The Army of the Commonweal," *Journal of Political Economy*, June, pp. 456–461.

"The Economic Theory of Woman's Dress," *Popular Science Monthly*, Nov., pp. 198–205.

1898

"Why Is Economics Not an Evolutionary Science?" *Quarterly Journal of Economics*, July, pp. 373–397.

"The Instinct of Workmanship and the Irksomeness of Labour," *American Journal of Sociology*, Sept., pp. 187–201.

"The Beginnings of Ownership," *American Journal of Sociology*, Nov., pp. 352–365.

"The Barbarian Status of Women," *American Journal of Sociology*, Jan., pp. 503–514.

1899

The Theory of the Leisure Class: an Economic Study of the Evolution of Institutions; title changed in 1912 to *The Theory of the Leisure Class: an Economic Study of Institutions,* New York, Macmillan Co.

"The Preconceptions of Economic Science," *Quarterly Journal of Economics,* Jan., pp. 121–150; July, pp. 396–426; Jan. 1900, pp. 240–269.

"Mr. Cummings's Strictures on *The Theory of the Leisure Class,*" *Journal of Political Economy,* Dec., pp. 106–117.

1900

"Industrial and Pecuniary Employments," *Publications of the American Economic Association,* Series 3, 1901, pp. 190–235.

1901

"Gustav Schmoller's Economics," *Quarterly Journal of Economics,* Nov., pp. 69–93.

1902

"Arts and Crafts," *Journal of Political Economy,* Dec., pp. 108–111.

1903

"The Use of Loan Credit in Modern Business," *Decennial Publications of the University of Chicago,* Series I, No. 4, pp. 31–50, republished without substantial change in *The Theory of Business Enterprise.*

1904

"An Early Experiment in Trusts," *Journal of Political Economy,* March, pp. 270–279.

The Theory of Business Enterprise, New York, C. Scribner's Sons.

1905

"Credit and Prices," *Journal of Political Economy*, June, pp. 460–472.

1906

"The Place of Science in Modern Civilisation," *American Journal of Sociology*, March, pp. 585–609.

"Professor Clark's Economics," *Quarterly Journal of Economics*, Feb., pp. 147–195.

"Socialist Economics of Karl Marx and His Followers," *Quarterly Journal of Economics*, Aug., pp. 578–595; Feb. 1907, pp. 299–322.

1907

"Fisher's Capital and Income," *Political Science Quarterly*, March, pp. 112–128.

1908

"The Evolution of the Scientific Point of View," *University of California Chronicle*, May, pp. 396–416.

"On the Nature of Capital," *Quarterly Journal of Economics*, Aug., pp. 517–542; Nov., pp. 104–136.

1909

"Fisher's Rate of Interest," *Political Science Quarterly*, June, pp. 296–303.

"The Limitations of Marginal Utility," *Journal of Political Economy*, Nov., pp. 620–636.

1910

"Christian Morals and the Competitive System," *International Journal of Ethics*, Jan., pp. 168–185.

"As to a Proposed Inquiry into Baltic and Cretan Antiquities," memorandum submitted to Carnegie Institution of Washington, published in *American Journal of Sociology*, Sept. 1933, pp. 237–241.

"The Mutation Theory, the Blond Race, and the Aryan Culture," paper submitted to Carnegie Institution of Washington and later elaborated into the two papers following:

1913

"The Mutation Theory and the Blond Race," *Journal of Race Development*, April, pp. 491–507.
"The Blond Race and the Aryan Culture," *University of Missouri Bulletin, Science Series*, Vol. 2, No. 3, April, pp. 39–57.

1914

The Instinct of Workmanship and the State of the Industrial Arts, New York, Macmillan Co.

1915

"The Opportunity of Japan," *Journal of Race Development*, July, pp. 23–38.
Imperial Germany and the Industrial Revolution, New York, Viking Press.

1917

An Inquiry into the Nature of Peace and the Terms of Its Perpetuation, New York, Macmillan Co.
"Suggestions Touching the Working Program of an Inquiry into the Prospective Terms of Peace," memorandum submitted to the House Inquiry, through Walter Lippmann, Dec., published in *Political Science Quarterly*, June 1932, pp. 186–189.
"An Outline of a Policy for the Control of the 'Economic Penetration' of Backward Countries and of Foreign Investments," memorandum for House Inquiry published in *Political Science Quarterly*, June 1932, pp. 189–203.

1918

"On the General Principles of a Policy of Reconstruction," *Journal of the National Institute of Social Sciences*, April, pp. 37–46; republished in part as

"A Policy of Reconstruction," *New Republic*, April 13, pp. 318–320.

Report ad interim to Raymond Pearl on trip through prairie states in behalf of Statistical Division of Food Administration, published in *American Economic Review*, Sept. 1933, pp. 478–479.

"Passing of National Frontiers," *Dial*, April 25, pp. 387–390.

"Using the I.W.W. to Harvest Grain," memorandum for Statistical Division of Food Administration, published in *Journal of Political Economy*, Dec. 1932, pp. 796–807.

"A Schedule of Prices for the Staple Foodstuffs," memorandum for Statistical Division of Food Administration, published in *Southwestern Social Science Quarterly*, March 1933, pp. 372–377.

"Menial Servants during the Period of the War," *Public*, May 11, pp. 595–599.

"The War and Higher Learning," *Dial*, July 18, pp. 45–49.

The Higher Learning in America, A Memorandum on the Conduct of Universities by Business Men, New York, B. W. Huebsch.

"Farm Labour and the Country Towns," memorandum for the Statistical Division of the Food Administration, published in an elaborated form as:

"Farm Labour for the Period of the War," *Public*, July 13, pp. 882–885; July 20, pp. 918–922; July 27, pp. 947–952; Aug. 3, pp. 981–985.

"The Modern Point of View and the New Order," *Dial*, Oct. 19, pp. 289–293; Nov. 22, pp. 349–354; Nov. 16, pp. 409–414; Nov. 30, pp. 482–488; Dec. 14, pp. 543–549; Dec. 28, pp. 605–611; Jan. 11, 1919, pp. 19–24; Jan. 25, pp. 75–82. Republished as:

1919

The Vested Interests and the State of the Industrial Arts; title changed in 1920 to *The Vested Interests and the Common Man*, New York, Viking Press.

"Bolshevism Is a Menace—to Whom?" *Dial*, Feb. 22, pp. 174–179.

"The Intellectual Pre-eminence of Jews in Modern Europe,"
Political Science Quarterly, March, pp. 33–42.
"On the Nature and Uses of Sabotage," *Dial*, April 5, pp. 341–
346.
"Peace," *Dial*, May 17, pp. 485–487.
"The Captains of Finance and the Engineers," *Dial*, June 14,
pp. 599–606.
"The Industrial System and the Captains of Industry," *Dial*,
May 31, pp. 552–557.
"Bolshevism and the Vested Interests in America," *Dial*,
Oct. 4, pp. 296–301; Oct. 18, pp. 339–346; Nov. 1, pp. 373–
380.
The Place of Science in Modern Civilisation and Other Essays,
New York, B. W. Huebsch.

1921

The Engineers and the Price System, New York, Viking Press.
"Between Bolshevism and War," *Freeman*, May 25, pp. 248–
251.

1922

"Dementia Praecox," *Freeman*, June 21, pp. 344–347.

1923

"The Captain of Industry," *Freeman*, April 18, pp. 127–132.
"The Timber Lands and Oil Fields," *Freeman*, May 23, pp.
248–250; May 30, pp. 272–274.
"The Independent Farmer," *Freeman*, June 13, pp. 321–324.
"The Country Town," *Freeman*, July 11, pp. 417–420; July 18,
pp. 440–443.
*Absentee Ownership and Business Enterprise in Recent Times;
the Case of America*, New York, B. W. Huebsch.

1925

"Economic Theory in the Calculable Future," *American Economic Review*, March, Supplement, pp. 48–55.
The Laxdaela Saga, translated from the Icelandic with an Introduction, New York, B. W. Huebsch.

1927

"An Experiment in Eugenics," published for the first time in *Essays in Our Changing Order*, New York, Viking Press, 1934.

SELECTED BIBLIOGRAPHY OF JOHN R. COMMONS

1891

The History of Higher Education in Ohio, with George W. Knight (*Bureau of Education Circular of Information No. 5; Contributions to American Educational History No. 12; whole number 175*), Washington, Government Printing Office.

1892

The Christian Minister and Sociology (Christian Social Union Publication No. 4), Baltimore, Guggenheimer, Weil and Co.
"Protection and Natural Monopolies," *Quarterly Journal of Economics,* July, pp. 479–484.

1893

The Distribution of Wealth, New York, Macmillan Co.
"The Church and the Problem of Poverty in the Cities," *Charities Review,* May, pp. 347–356.

1894

Social Reform and the Church, introduction by Richard T. Ely, New York, Crowell and Co.

1895

"State Supervision for Cities," *Annals of the American Academy of Political and Social Science,* May, pp. 865–881.
"Taxation in Chicago and Philadelphia," *Journal of Political Economy,* Sept., pp. 434–460.

1896

Proportional Representation (Library of Economics and Politics, No. 8, edited by R. T. Ely), New York, Crowell and Co.

1897

"A Comparison of Day Labor and Contract System on Municipal Works," *American Federationist,* Jan.–Feb., pp. 229–232, 252–254; March–Dec., pp. 3–6, 27–29, 49–51, 71–73, 88–90, 111–113, 150–154, 183–186, 207–209, 229–231; Jan., 1898, pp. 252–253. In *Yale Review* under title, "The Day Labor and Contract Systems on Municipal Works," Feb., pp. 428–445.
"Natural Selection, Social Selection, and Heredity," *The Arena,* July, pp. 90–97.
"The Junior Republic I," *American Journal of Sociology,* Nov., pp. 281–296.
"Municipal Electric Lighting," *Municipal Affairs,* Dec., pp. 631–673.

1898

"The Junior Republic II," *American Journal of Sociology,* Jan., pp. 433–448.
"The Value of the Study of Political Economy to the Christian Minister," *Methodist Review,* Sept., pp. 696–711.
"Social Economics and City Evangelization," *The Christian City,* Dec., pp. 767–772.

1899

"The Right to Work," *The Arena,* Feb., pp. 131–142.
Proportional Representation, Study No. II (Publications of the Social Reform Union), Oct., Alhambra, California.
"A Sociological View of Sovereignty," *American Journal of Sociology,* July–Nov., pp. 1–15, 155–171, 347–366; Jan.–May 1900, pp. 544–552, 683–695, 814–825; July 1900, pp. 67–89.

1900

Representative Democracy, New York, Bureau of Economic Research.
"Municipal Employment and Progress," *Municipal Affairs,* June, pp. 294–316.
"Representation of Interests," *The Independent,* June 21, pp. 1479–1483.
"Index Numbers of Prices, Freight Rates, Etc.," *Quarterly Bulletin of the Bureau of Economic Research,* July, pp. 1–34.
"Wholesale Prices 1896 to 1900," *Quarterly Bulletin of the Bureau of Economic Research,* Oct., pp. 35–54.

1901

Reports of the Industrial Commission on Immigration and Education, U. S. Government Report, Vol. XV, pp. 1–41, Washington, Government Printing Office.
"A New Way of Settling Labor Disputes," *American Monthly Review of Reviews,* March, pp. 328–333.
"Municipal Administration of Public Utilities," *The Independent,* Nov. 7, pp. 2633–2636.

1902

Final Report of the Industrial Commission, U. S. Government Report, Vol. XIX, pp. 977–1030, 1085–1113, Washington, Government Printing Office.
Proportional Representation: The Gerrymander, Girard, Kansas.
"The Physical Vigor of Public Employees," *Yale Review,* Feb., pp. 416–423.
"Economic and Social Factors in Chicago Municipal Lighting," *Municipal Affairs,* March, pp. 109–115.
"Wages in Municipal Employment," *Quarterly Journal of Economics,* May, pp. 433–450.
"Symposium on Concentration of Wealth: Its Dangers," *The Independent,* May 1, pp. 1040–1044.

Mortgage Taxation (Bulletin No. I), New York, Taxation Department, National Civic Federation.

"Referendum and Initiative in City Government," *Political Science Quarterly*, Dec., pp. 609–630.

1903

Bulletin of the National Civic Federation (*Taxation Department Bulletin* No. 2), New York, Jan., pp. 1–11.

"Some Taxation Problems and Reforms," *American Monthly Review of Reviews*, Feb., pp. 202–208.

" 'Welfare Work' in a Great Industrial Plant," *American Monthly Review of Reviews*, July, pp. 79–81.

"The Present Status of the American Labor Movement," *American Monthly Review of Reviews*, Aug., pp. 177–180. In *Public Opinion*, Aug. 6, pp. 175–176.

Racial Composition of the American People, series of nine articles, *The Chautauquan*, Sept.–Dec., pp. 33–42, 118–125, 223–234, 333–340; Jan.–Feb., 1904, pp. 433–443, 533–543; March–May, 1904, pp. 13–22, 115–124, 217–225.

1904

"Report on Regulation and Restriction of Output," in collaboration with others, *Eleventh Special Report of the Commissioner of Labor, H. R. Document No. 734*, 58th Congress, 2d Session, Washington, Government Printing Office.

"The New York Building Trades," *Quarterly Journal of Economics*, May, pp. 409–434.

"Arbitration, Conciliation, Trade Agreement," *The Independent*, June 23, pp. 1440–1444. In *Public Policy*, Sept. 17, pp. 141–144.

"Labor Conditions in Meat Packing and the Recent Strike," *Quarterly Journal of Economics*, Nov., pp. 1–32.

"Slavs in the Bituminous Mines of Illinois," *The Charities*, Dec. 3, pp. 227–229.

1905

"Causes of the Union-Shop Policy," paper presented at 17th annual meeting of American Economic Association, Chicago. In *Publications of the American Economic Association,* 3rd series, Vol. VI, pp. 140–159.

Trade Unionism and Labor Problems, John R. Commons, editor; author in collaboration with associates; writer of introduction, New York, Ginn and Co.

"Types of American Labor Organization—The Teamsters of Chicago," *Quarterly Journal of Economics,* May, pp. 400–433.

"Types of American Labor Unions: The Longshoremen of the Great Lakes," *Quarterly Journal of Economics,* Nov., pp. 59–85.

1906

"Conciliation in the Stove Industry," with J. P. Frey, U. S. Government Report, Department of Commerce and Labor *(Bulletin of the Bureau of Labor No. 62)*, Jan., pp. 124–196.

"Types of American Labor Unions—The Musicians of St. Louis and New York," *Quarterly Journal of Economics,* May, pp. 419–442.

1907

"Labor and Politics," in *Municipal and Private Operations of Public Utilities; Report to the National Civic Federation Commission on Public Ownership and Operation,* Part I, Vol. I, New York, National Civic Federation, pp. 88–112.

"Labor and Politics: United States Water Works; United States Gas Works; United States Electricity Works; United States Water, Gas and Electricity Works Supplementary Comments," with J. W. Sullivan, in *Municipal and Private Operation of Public Utilities; Report to the National Civic Federation Commission on Public Ownership and Operation,* Part II, Vol. I, New York, National Civic Federation, pp. 136–158, 490–536, 749–758, 885–908.

"Labor Organization and Labor Politics—1827–37," *Quarterly Journal of Economics,* Feb., pp. 323–329.

"The Wisconsin Public-Utilities Law," *American Review of Reviews,* Aug., pp. 221–224.

"Political Economy and Business Economy: Comments on Fisher's Capital and Income," *Quarterly Journal of Economics*, Nov., pp. 120–125.

1908

Races and Immigrants in America, New York, Macmillan Co.
"The Single Tax in Theory and Practice," *The Public*, March, pp. 1205–1209.
"Is Class Conflict in America Growing and Is It Inevitable?" address delivered before American Sociological Society, Dec. 1906. In *American Journal of Sociology*, May, pp. 756–766, 781–783.
"Robert Marion LaFollette," *North American Review*, May, pp. 672–677.
"Tariff Revision and Protection for American Labor," *Annals of the American Academy of Political and Social Science*, Sept., pp. 315–320.
"The International Association for Labor Legislation," *Charities and the Commons*, Sept. 12, pp. 687–689.
"Standardizing the Home," address delivered before American Home Economics Association, Boston, Dec. 1909. In *Publications of the American Statistical Association* under title "Standardization of Housing Investigations," Dec., pp. 319–326.

1909

"Trade Schools and University Extension for Wisconsin," *LaFollette's Magazine*, Jan. 30, pp. 12–13.
"Wage Earners of Pittsburgh," *Charities and the Commons*, March 6, pp. 1051–1064.
"Workingmen's Accident Insurance," *LaFollette's Magazine*, March 6, pp. 8–9.
"Workmen's Accident Insurance," *Charities and the Commons*, March 27, pp. 1259–1262.
"Horace Greeley and the Working Class Origins of the Republican Party," *Political Science Quarterly*, Sept., pp. 468–488.
"American Shoemakers, 1648–1895: A Sketch of Industrial

Evolution," *Quarterly Journal of Economics,* Nov., pp. 39–84.

"Utilitarian Idealism," *Intercollegiate Magazine,* Dec., pp. 267–269.

Administration of Labor Laws by C. B. Austin, introduction by John R. Commons; *Woman's Work* by Maud Swett, introduction by John R. Commons; *Child Labor* by Laura Scott (*Summary of Labor Laws in Force 1909, Legislative Reviews* Nos. 3, 4, 5 (1910), prepared under direction of John R. Commons), New York, American Association for Labor Legislation.

1910

A Documentary History of American Industrial Society, edited by John R. Commons, U. B. Phillips, E. A. Gilmore, H. L. Sumner, and J. B. Andrews, 10 vols., Cleveland, Arthur H. Clark Co.

"A Score Card for Houses," *Wisconsin Alumni Magazine,* Jan., pp. 148–153.

"How Wisconsin Regulates Her Public Utilities," *American Review of Reviews,* Aug., pp. 215–217.

1911

Proposed Minimum Wage Law for Wisconsin, prepared for the Wisconsin Consumers' League under the direction of Commons.

"Organized Labor's Attitude Toward Industrial Efficiency," *American Economic Review,* Sept., pp. 463–472.

"The Industrial Commission of Wisconsin," address delivered before American Association for Labor Legislation at Chicago. In *American Labor Legislation Review,* Dec., pp. 61–69.

1912

Eighteen Months' Work of the Milwaukee Bureau of Economy and Efficiency (*Milwaukee Bureau of Economy and Efficiency Bulletin* No. 19), April, Milwaukee, Wisconsin.

Findings of the [Wisconsin Industrial] Commission, Madison, Wisconsin, April, pp. 7–18.

1913

Labor and Administration, New York, Macmillan Co.

"Industrial Education and Dependency," address delivered before Social Service Institute. As *Bulletin of the University of Wisconsin* Serial No. 579, July, Madison, Wisconsin, Extension Division of University of Wisconsin.

The Industrial Commission of Wisconsin: Its Organization and Methods, Madison, Wisconsin, Industrial Commission of Wisconsin. In *The Survey*, under the title, "Constructive Investigation and the Industrial Commission of Wisconsin," Jan. 4, pp. 440–448.

"How the Wisconsin Industrial Commission Works," address delivered before sixth annual meeting of the American Association for Labor Legislation. In *American Labor Legislation Review*, Feb., pp. 9–14.

Testimony concerning H. R. 22593, a bill dealing with valuation of several classes of common carriers, on Feb. 13–14, 17, in *Physical Valuation of Common Carriers: Hearings before the Committee on Interstate Commerce, U. S. Senate*, Washington, Government Printing Office, pp. 83–153.

1914

"Proportional Representation," address delivered before Municipal League. In *Municipal League Bulletin*, Sept., pp. 6–10.

1915

"Social Insurance and the Medical Profession," address delivered before the sixty-eighth annual meeting of State Medical Society of Wisconsin, Oct. 1914. In *Wisconsin Medical Journal*, Jan., pp. 301–306.

1916

Principles of Labor Legislation, with J. B. Andrews, New York, Harper and Bros.

"Report of Commissioners John R. Commons and Florence J. Harriman," in *Industrial Relations: Final Report and Testimony Submitted to Congress by the Commission on Industrial Relations*, Senate Document No. 415, 64th Congress, 1st session, Vol. I, Washington, Government Printing Office, pp. 171–230.

"Unemployment and Its Relation to Businessmen's Organizations," paper presented at First Commercial and Industrial Congress at Madison, Wisconsin. In *Bulletin of the University of Wisconsin*, No. 800, July, pp. 77–88.

1917

"Eight-Hour Shifts by Federal Legislation," address delivered before tenth annual meeting of the American Association for Labor Legislation, Dec. 1916. In *American Labor Legislation Review*, March, pp. 139–154.

1918

History of Labour in the United States, with D. J. Saposs, H. L. Sumner, E. B. Mittleman, H. E. Hoagland, J. B. Andrews, and Selig Perlman, 4 vols., New York, Macmillan Co.

"Balance of Power by Disarmament," *American Review of Reviews*, Feb., pp. 177–181.

German Socialists and the War, New York, American Alliance for Labor and Democracy.

"Economic Reconstruction: Foreign and Domestic Investments," annual address of the president of the American Economic Association, Dec. 1917. In *American Economic Review Supplement*, March, pp. 5–17.

"Health Insurance," address delivered before the seventy-second annual meeting of State Medical Society of Wisconsin. In *Wisconsin Medical Journal*, Nov., pp. 218–223.

1919

Industrial Goodwill, New York, McGraw-Hill Book Co.

"The Health Insurance Movement in the United States—Appendix A," with A. J. Altmeyer, in *Health, Health In-*

surance, *Old Age Pensions,* Columbus, Ohio, Ohio Health
and Old Age Insurance Commission, Feb., pp. 287–311.
"The Health Insurance Movement in the United States—Special Report XVI," with A. J. Altmeyer, in *Report of the
Health Insurance Commission of the State of Illinois,* May,
pp. 625–647.
"A Reconstruction Health Program," *The Survey,* Sept. 6,
pp. 798–801.

1920

Races and Immigrants in America, new edition, New York,
Macmillan Co.
"What's Wrong with Labor? A . . . Study of the Experiments
in Industrial Government . . . ; Series of Articles . . . on
the Big Plants that Are Finding a Way Out of Labor Trou-
bles," in collaboration with associates, *The Independent,*
April–June, pp. 3–5, 28–30, 160–161, 189–191, 317, 340–341;
July–Sept., pp. 7, 32, 73–74, 94, 137–138, 163–164, 301, 313–
315; Oct.–Dec., pp. 5–6, 33, 184, 202–204, 325, 344–347; Jan.–
Feb., 1921, pp. 61, 76–78, 179–180, 196–198.
"Health Programs," address delivered before the fifteenth annual meeting of the National Tuberculosis Association in
1919. As *Bulletin of the University of Wisconsin* Serial No.
1055, under the title, *A Reconstruction Health Program,*
June, Madison, Wisconsin, University Extension Division.

1921

Industrial Government, with Willis Wisler, A. P. Haake, O. F.
Carpenter, J. M. Turner, E. B. Dietrich, Jean Davis, and
Malcolm Sharp, New York, Macmillan Co.
Trade Unionism and Labor Problems, second series edition,
John R. Commons, editor; author in collaboration with as-
sociates; writer of introduction, New York, Ginn and Co.
"The Webbs' Constitution for the Socialist Commonwealth,"
American Economic Review, March, pp. 82–90.
"Unemployment: Compensation and Prevention," *The Sur-
vey,* Oct. 1, pp. 5–9.

1922

"Unemployment Insurance," *The Monitor,* Feb., pp. 2–7.
"A Progressive Tax on Bare Land Values," *Political Science Quarterly,* March, pp. 41–68.
"Unemployment Prevention," *American Labor Legislation Review,* March, pp. 15–24.
"Industrial Government," *Railway Expressman,* June, pp. 33–36.
"Les tendances du mouvement syndical aux Etats-Unis," *Revue Internationale du Travail,* June, pp. 919–955. This article appeared also in an English version of the same periodical issue, pp. 855–887.
"Secular Trend and Business Cycles," with H. L. McCracken and W. E. Zeuch, *Review of Economic Statistics,* Oct., pp. 244–263.

1923

"Unemployment: Prevention and Insurance," in *The Stabilization of Business,* edited by L. D. Edie, New York, Macmillan Co., pp. 164–205.
Unemployment Insurance, Madison, Wisconsin, Wisconsin Association for the Prevention of Unemployment.
"Wage Theories and Wage Policies," paper presented at the thirty-fifth annual meeting of the American Economic Association. In *American Economic Review Supplement,* March, pp. 110–117.
"Radicalism and the Farm Bloc," *North American Review,* April, pp. 443–448.
"Hobson's 'Economics of Unemployment,' " *American Economic Review,* Dec., pp. 638–647.

1924

Legal Foundations of Capitalism, New York, Macmillan Co.
State Minimum Wage Laws in Practice, with Felix Frankfurter and Mary W. Dewson, New York, National Consumers' League.

"The Delivered Price Practice in the Steel Market," *American Economic Review*, Sept., pp. 505–519.

"La Follette and Wisconsin," *The New Republic*, Sept. 17, pp. 63–65.

1925

Can Business Prevent Unemployment? with S. A. Lewisohn, E. G. Draper, and D. D. Lescohier, New York, Alfred A. Knopf.

"Law and Economics," *Yale Law Journal*, Feb., pp. 371–382.

"The Passing of Samuel Gompers," *Current History*, Feb., pp. 670–676.

"The Stabilization of Prices and Business," *American Economic Review*, March, pp. 43–52.

"The True Scope of Unemployment Insurance," *American Labor Legislation Review*, March, pp. 33–44.

"Capitalism and Socialism," address delivered before the Wisconsin State Bar Association. In *Proceedings of the Wisconsin State Bar Association*, pp. 62–82.

"Marx Today: Capitalism and Socialism," *Atlantic Monthly*, Nov., pp. 682–693.

1926

"Karl Marx and Samuel Gompers," *Political Science Quarterly*, June, pp. 281–286.

1927

Testimony concerning H. R. 7895 and H. R. 11806, Strong bills, to amend portions of the Federal Reserve Act to define the policies of the Federal Reserve Act and to provide for the stabilization of the price level for commodities in general. In *Stabilization: Hearings before the House Committee on Banking and Currency*, 69th Congress, 1st session, Washington, Government Printing Office, Feb., pp. 1074–1121.

"Workers Education and the Universities," *American Federationist*, April, pp. 424–426.

"Price Stabilization and the Federal Reserve System," *The Annalist*, April 1, pp. 459–462.
"Reserve Bank Control of the General Price Level: A Rejoinder," *The Annalist*, July 8, pp. 43–44.
"Legal and Economic Job Analysis," with E. W. Morehouse, *Yale Law Journal*, Dec., pp. 139–178.

1928

"Farm Prices and the Value of Gold," *North American Review*, Jan.–Feb., pp. 27–41, 196–211.

1929

"Jurisdictional Disputes," as Lecture IV in *Wertheim Lectures on Industrial Relations*, Cambridge, Harvard University Press, pp. 93–123.
Testimony concerning S. Res. 219, a resolution providing for an analysis and appraisal of reports on unemployment and systems for prevention and relief thereof, in *Unemployment in the United States: Hearings before the Committee on Education and Labor, U. S. Senate*, 70th Congress, 2nd session, Washington, Government Printing Office, Feb., pp. 212–270.
Agricultural Tariffs, with B. H. Hibbard and S. Perlman, Freeport, Illinois, Rawleigh.

1930

"Economic Basis of Progress for Personal Finance," *American Association of Personal Finance Companies, Yearbook*, pp. 173–183.
"Evaluating Institutions as a Factor in Economic Change," *U.S.D.A. Graduate School Special Lectures on Economics*, Washington, Feb.–March, pp. 7–22.
"Unemployment Compensation," address delivered before the 1930 Convention of Wisconsin Federation of Labor. In *American Labor Legislation Review*, Sept., pp. 249–253.
"Unemployment Reserves and Unemployment Insurance," *American Labor Legislation Review*, Sept., pp. 266–268.

1931

"Should America Adopt a System of Compulsory Unemployment Insurance?" *Congressional Digest; Special Annual Debate Number*, Washington, Aug.–Sept., pp. 214, 216.
"Institutional Economics," *American Economic Review*, Dec., pp. 648–657.
Economic Survey of Wisconsin, in collaboration with associates. Published in two parts as follows:
Statistical Summary of an Economic Survey of Wisconsin, Madison, Wisconsin, Dec.
Part II: Agriculture Credit, Madison, Wisconsin, March, 1932.

1932

"Labor Movement," "Edward Kellogg," and "Herman Justi," in *Encyclopaedia of the Social Sciences*, edited by E. R. A. Seligman and Alvin Johnson, New York, Macmillan Co., Vol. VIII, pp. 682–696, 556–557, 507–508.
"The Groves Unemployment Reserves Law," *American Labor Legislation Review*, March, pp. 8–10.
"Unemployment Insurance," address delivered over NBC network as part of economic series sponsored by National Advisory Council on Radio in Education. As *Economic Series Lecture* No. 24, Chicago, University of Chicago Press.
"What Is the Difference Between Unemployment Insurance and Unemployment Reserves?" *State Government*, May, pp. 3–5.
"Comment by Professor Commons," *American Economic Review*, June, pp. 264–268.
"The Problem of Correlating Law, Economics and Ethics," *Wisconsin Law Review*, Dec., pp. 3–26.

1933

"Editors' Introduction," with B. H. Hibbard and W. A. Morton, in Lippert S. Ellis, *The Tariff on Sugar*, Freeport, Illinois, Rawleigh Foundation, pp. 13–22.
"Editors' Introduction," with B. H. Hibbard and W. A. Mor-

ton, in R. R. Renne, *The Tariff on Dairy Products*, Madison, Wisconsin, Tariff Research Committee, pp. 15–22.

"Materialistic, Psychological, Institutional Economics," in *Economic Essays in Honour of Gustav Cassel*, London, George Allen and Unwin, pp. 89–103.

"Editors' Introduction," with B. H. Hibbard and W. A. Morton, in T. W. Schultz, *The Tariff on Barley, Oats and Corn*, Madison, Wisconsin, Tariff Research Committee, pp. v–x.

1934

Institutional Economics; Its Place in Political Economy, New York, Macmillan Co.

Myself, New York, Macmillan Co.

1935

"The Gold Clause Decisions," *Economic Forum*, Spring, pp. 23–34.

"New Deal and Teaching of Economics," impromptu address delivered before the forty-seventh annual meeting of the American Economic Association, Dec. 1934. In *American Economic Review Supplement*, March, pp. 10–11.

"Communism and Collective Democracy," *American Economic Review*, June, pp. 212–223.

"The Place of Economics in Social Philosophy," *Journal of Social Philosophy*, Oct., pp. 7–22.

1936

"Institutional Economics," *American Economic Review Supplement*, March, pp. 237–249.

1937

"Capacity to Produce, Capacity to Consume, Capacity to Pay Debts," *American Economic Review*, Dec., pp. 680–697.

1938

"What I Saw in the Tennessee Valley," *Survey Graphic*, May, pp. 279–281.

1939

"Twentieth Century Economics," *Journal of Social Philosophy*, Oct., pp. 29–41.

1942

"Legislative and Administrative Reasoning in Economics," *Journal of Farm Economics*, May, pp. 369–391.

SELECTED BIBLIOGRAPHY OF WESLEY C. MITCHELL

1896

"The Quantity Theory of the Value of Money," *Journal of Political Economy*, March, pp. 139–165.

"The New Gold and the Fall of Prices," *Journal of Political Economy*, Dec., pp. 84–85.

1897

"Greenbacks and the Cost of the Civil War," *Journal of Political Economy*, March, pp. 117–156.

1898

"The Value of the 'Greenbacks' during the Civil War," *Journal of Political Economy*, March, pp. 139–167.

"Resumption of Specie Payments in Austria-Hungary," *Journal of Political Economy*, Dec., pp. 106–113.

1899

"The Suspension of Specie Payments, December 1861," *Journal of Political Economy*, June, pp. 289–326.

1900

"Preparations for the Twelfth Census," *Journal of Political Economy*, June, pp. 378–384.

"The Inheritance Tax Decision," *Journal of Political Economy*, June, pp. 387–397.

"The Census of Cuba," *Journal of Political Economy,* Dec., pp. 125–131.

1901

"The Census of Porto Rico," *Journal of Political Economy,* March, pp. 282–285.

Five articles on the 1901 steel strike, *Chicago Tribune.* "Industrial Status of the Steel Strike," July 21, p. 2, and July 22, p. 3; "Employers' Attitude in the Steel Strike," July 23, p. 2; "Steel Strikers' Claims for Recognition," July 24, p. 2; "Effect of Steel Strike on 'The Public,' " July 27, p. 2.

1902

"The Circulating Medium during the Civil War," *Journal of Political Economy,* Sept., pp. 537–574.

1903

A History of the Greenbacks, with Special Reference to the Economic Consequences of Their Issue: 1862–65, Chicago, University of Chicago Press.

1904

"The Real Issues in the Quantity Theory Controversy," *Journal of Political Economy,* June, pp. 403–408.

1905

"Occupation Statistics of the Twelfth Census," *Quarterly Publications of the American Statistical Association,* June, pp. 231–238.

"Methods of Presenting Statistics of Wages," *Quarterly Publications of the American Statistical Association,* Dec., pp. 325–343.

1908

Gold, Prices, and Wages under the Greenback Standard, University of California Publications in Economics, Vol. 1.

1909

"The Course of Prices from 1893 to 1908," *Journal of Commerce and Commercial Bulletin*, Jan. 4, p. 5.
"The British Board of Trade's Investigations into Cost of Living," *Quarterly Journal of Economics*, Feb., pp. 345–350.
"The Decline in the Ratio of Banking Capital to Liabilities," *Quarterly Journal of Economics*, Aug., pp. 697–713.

1910

"The Rationality of Economic Activity," *Journal of Political Economy*, Feb. and March, pp. 97–113, 197–216.
"The Prices of American Stocks: 1890–1909," *Journal of Political Economy*, May, pp. 345–380.
"The Prices of Preferred and Common Stocks: 1890–1909," *Journal of Political Economy*, July, pp. 513–524.
"The Dun-Gibson Index Number," *Quarterly Journal of Economics*, Nov., pp. 161–172.

1911

"Rates of Interest and the Prices of Investment Securities: 1890–1909," *Journal of Political Economy*, April, pp. 269–308.
"The Publications of the National Monetary Commission," *Quarterly Journal of Economics*, May, pp. 563–593.
"The Trustworthiness of the Bureau of Labor's Index Number of Wages," *Quarterly Journal of Economics*, May, pp. 613–620.
"The British Report upon Real Wages in America and England," *Quarterly Journal of Economics*, Nov., pp. 160–163.

1912

"The Backward Art of Spending Money," *American Economic Review*, June, pp. 269–281.

1913

"Security Prices and Interest Rates in 1910–12," *Journal of Political Economy*, June, pp. 500–522.
Business Cycles, Berkeley, University of California Press.

1914

"The New Banking Measure in the United States," *Economic Journal*, March, pp. 130–138.

"Human Behavior and Economics: A Survey of Recent Literature," *Quarterly Journal of Economics*, Nov., pp. 1–47.

"Economics," *American Year Book*, pp. 672–673.

1915

"How the Statistical Output of Federal Bureaus Might Be Improved," *Quarterly Publications of the American Statistical Association*, March, pp. 422–424.

"The Making and Using of Index Numbers," Part I of *Index Numbers of Wholesale Prices in the United States and Foreign Countries*, Bulletin of the U. S. Bureau of Labor Statistics, No. 173, July, pp. 5–114.

"Economics," *American Year Book*, pp. 667–668.

1916

"American Security Prices and Interest Rates, by Months, January 1913 to December 1915; by Years, 1890–1915," *Journal of Political Economy*, Feb., pp. 126–157.

"The Role of Money in Economic Theory," *American Economic Review*, March, pp. 140–161.

"A Critique of Index Numbers of the Prices of Stocks," *Journal of Political Economy*, July, pp. 625–693.

"Economics," *American Year Book*, pp. 347–348.

1917

"Wieser's Theory of Social Economics," *Political Science Quarterly*, March, pp. 95–118.

"Economics," *American Year Book*, pp. 325–326.

1918

Discussion of Carleton H. Parker's paper, "Motives in Economic Life," *American Economic Review*, March, Supplement, pp. 235–237.

"Bentham's Felicific Calculus," *Political Science Quarterly*, June, pp. 161–183.

"Our Memorial Volume," *Quarterly Publications of the American Statistical Association,* Sept., pp. 119–120.

"War Prices in the United States," *Economic Journal,* Dec., pp. 460–463.

"Economics," *American Year Book,* p. 380.

1919

"Report of the Committee on the Purchasing Power of Money in Relation to the War," with others, *American Economic Review,* March, Supplement, pp. 364–365.

"Increase in the Production of Raw Materials, 1913–1918," *Federal Reserve Bulletin,* April 1, pp. 336–337.

"Statistics and Government," *Quarterly Publications of the American Statistical Association,* March, pp. 223–235.

"Sound Money Doctrine," a review of J. L. Laughlin's *Money and Prices.* In *Nation,* Sept. 13, pp. 376–377.

"Economics," *American Year Book,* pp. 738–739.

A Comparison of Prices during the Civil War and Present War, Price Section, Division of Planning and Statistics, War Industries Board, Government Printing Office.

History of Prices during the War (editor in chief), U. S. War Industries Board, Price Bulletins Nos. 1–57, Government Printing Office, 1919–1920.

History of Prices during the War, Summary, U. S. War Industries Board, Price Bulletin No. 1, Government Printing Office.

History of Prices during the War, International Price Comparisons, assisted by Margaret L. Goldsmith and Florence K. Middaugh, U. S. War Industries Board, Price Bulletin No. 2, Government Printing Office.

1920

"Prices and Reconstruction," *American Economic Review,* March, Supplement, pp. 129–155.

"Report of the Joint Census Advisory Committee of the American Statistical and American Economic Associations," with others, *Quarterly Publications of the American Statistical Association,* March, pp. 76–107.

"The New School for Social Research," *New York Evening Post*, April 8, p. 8.

"The International Factor in Price Fluctuations," *Proceedings of the Academy of Political Science*, June, pp. 67–69.

"Second Report of the Advisory Committee on the Census," with others, *Quarterly Publications of the American Statistical Association*, Dec., pp. 465–483.

"One Price for Each Commodity versus a Graded Scale of Prices," a memorandum in Paul Willard Garrett's *Government Control over Prices*, U. S. War Industries Board, Price Bulletin No. 3, Government Printing Office.

1921

Testimony before the Committee on Education and Labor. In "Relieving Periods of Unemployment by a System of Public Works," Hearing on S.2749, to prepare for future cyclical periods of depression and unemployment by systems of public works, Dec. 21 and 22, 67th Congress, 2nd Session, pp. 4–8.

"Report upon the Apportionment of Representatives," with others, *Quarterly Publications of the American Statistical Association*, Dec., pp. 1004–1013.

Income in the United States: Its Amount and Distribution, 1909–1919, with Willford I. King, Frederick R. Macaulay, and Oswald W. Knauth, Vol. 1, Summary, New York, Harcourt, Brace and Co.

1922

Income in the United States: Its Amount and Distribution, 1909–1919 (editor), Vol. 2, Detailed Report, New York, National Bureau of Economic Research.

Second Annual Report of the Director of Research, New York, National Bureau of Economic Research, Feb., published, with minor revisions, as *A Bold Experiment: The Story of the National Bureau of Economic Research*.

"The Crisis of 1920 and the Problem of Controlling Business Cycles," *American Economic Review*, March, Supplement, pp. 20–32.

"Third Report of the Advisory Committee on the Census," with others, *Journal of the American Statistical Association,* March, pp. 82–98.

"The Business Cycle and Credits," *Robert Morris Associates Monthly Bulletin,* Dec., pp. 244–257.

"The Financial Policy in Its Relation to the Price Level," in *Report of the National Agricultural Conference,* House Document No. 195, 67th Congress, 2nd Session, Government Printing Office, pp. 70–74.

1923

"Making Goods and Making Money," *Mechanical Engineering,* Jan., pp. 4–6.

"Unemployment and Business Fluctuations," *American Labor Legislation Review,* March, pp. 15–22.

"Accountants and Economics with Reference to the Business Cycle," *Journal of Accountancy,* March, pp. 161–171.

"Final Report of the Joint Committee of the American Statistical and the American Economic Associations to the Director of the Census, 1922," with others, *Journal of the American Statistical Association,* March, pp. 628–649.

Business Cycles and Unemployment, with others, an investigation under the auspices of the National Bureau of Economic Research made for a Committee of the President's Conference on Unemployment, New York, McGraw-Hill Book Co.

"The Problem of Controlling Business Cycles," in *The Stabilization of Business,* edited by Lionel D. Edie, New York, Macmillan Co., pp. 1–53.

1924

"The Business Hazard in the Machine Tool Industry," *American Machinist,* Jan. 3, pp. 1–4.

"Report of the Representatives of the American Economic Association on the Social Science Research Council," with Horace Secrist, *American Economic Review,* March, Supplement, pp. 174–176.

"The Prospects of Economics," in *The Trend of Economics,*

edited by Rexford G. Tugwell, New York, Alfred A. Knopf, pp. 3–34.

1925

"Quantitative Analysis in Economic Theory," *American Economic Review*, March, pp. 1–12.

1926

"The Contribution of the Social Sciences in Solving Social Problems," *American Labor Legislation Review*, March, pp. 84–85.

1927

A discussion of Frank A. Fetter's paper, "Interest Theory and Price Movements," *American Economic Review*, March, Supplement, pp. 108–111.

"Economic Activity," *Saturday Review of Literature*, May 28, pp. 855–857.

"The Problem of Business Instability," *Proceedings of the Academy of Political Science*, July, pp. 649–650.

"Report of the Chairman," in *The Social Science Research Council Third Annual Report*, pp. 13–43.

Business Cycles: The Problem and Its Setting, New York, National Bureau of Economic Research.

Contribution to round table discussion of "Present Status and Future Prospects of Quantitative Economics," *American Economic Review*, March, Supplement, pp. 39–41.

1929

"Sombart's Hochkapitalismus," *Quarterly Journal of Economics*, Feb., pp. 303–323.

"Testing Business Cycles," *News-Bulletin of the National Bureau of Economic Research*, March 1, pp. 1–8.

"Americans All," *Survey*, June 1, pp. 296–300, 320–323.

"Allyn Abbott Young," *Journal of the American Statistical Association*, June, pp. 200–201.

"Thorstein Veblen, 1857–1929," *New Republic*, Sept. 4, pp. 66–68.

"Thorstein Veblen: 1857–1929," *Economic Journal*, Dec., pp. 646–650.

"Postulates and Preconceptions of Ricardian Economics," in *Essays in Philosophy*, edited by Thomas V. Smith and William K. Wright, Chicago, The Open Court Publishing Co., pp. 37–59.

Recent Economic Changes in the United States, with others, an investigation under the auspices of the National Bureau of Economic Research made for the Committee on Recent Economic Changes, of the President's Conference on Unemployment, 2 vols., New York, National Bureau of Economic Research.

1930

"Are There Practicable Steps toward an Industrial Equilibrium?" *Bulletin of the Taylor Society*, Feb., pp. 2–6.

"Business Cycles," in *Encyclopaedia of the Social Sciences*, Vol. III, pp. 92–107.

"Institutes for Research in the Social Sciences," *Journal of Proceedings and Addresses of the Association of American Universities, Thirty-first Annual Conference, November 1929*, Chicago, University of Chicago Press.

"Research in the Social Sciences," in *The New Social Science*, edited by Leonard D. White, Chicago, University of Chicago Press, pp. 4–15.

1931

"Engineering, Economics, and the Problem of Social Well-Being: The Economist's View," *Mechanical Engineering*, Feb., pp. 105–110.

"Henry Rogers Seager: 1870–1930," *Journal of the American Statistical Association*, March, pp. 83–84.

"Discussion: Causes of Depression," *Proceedings of the Academy of Political Science*, June, pp. 397–400.

"In Memory of Henry R. Seager," Introduction to Henry R. Seager's *Labor and Other Economic Essays*, edited by Charles A. Gulick, Jr., New York, Harper and Bros.

Letter to John M. Clark, Aug. 9, 1928, in *Methods in Social*

Science: A Case Book, edited by Stuart A. Rice, Chicago, University of Chicago Press, pp. 675–680.

"What Is Stabilization?" in *Possibilities of Business and Employment Stabilization,* Washington, Chamber of Commerce of the United States, pp. 7–14.

"The Economic Basis for Social Progress," *Proceedings of the National Conference of Social Work, Fifty-seventh Annual Meeting, June 1930,* Chicago, University of Chicago Press, pp. 34–49.

"Economics," in *A Quarter Century of Learning, 1904–1929,* edited by Dixon R. Fox, New York, Columbia University Press, pp. 31–61.

1933

"Business Cycles: The Story of Rhythms in the Money-Making World," *The World Today: Encyclopædia Britannica,* Vol. I, pp. 27–28.

"Alfred Marshall," in *Encyclopaedia of the Social Sciences,* Vol. X, pp. 155–157.

"The Application of Economic Knowledge," in *The Obligation of Universities to the Social Order,* New York, New York University Press, pp. 169–176, 204–205.

Recent Social Trends in the United States, with others, Report of the President's Research Committee on Social Trends, Wesley C. Mitchell, Chairman, 2 vols., New York, McGraw-Hill Book Co.

"Studies of Cyclical Behavior: A Progress Report from the National Bureau of Economic Research," in *Der Stand und die Nächste Zukunft der Konjunkturforschung: Festschrift für Arthur Spiethoff,* Munich, Duncker und Humblot, pp. 181–189.

1934

"America's Monetary Problems: Introduction," *Proceedings of the Academy of Political Science,* April, pp. 1–2.

Address in a symposium on "Economics in a Changing Social Order," with Willard E. Atkins and Isador Lubin. Delivered October 4, in the Economics Series sponsored by the Economics Committee of the National Advisory Council on Radio in Education in cooperation with the League for Industrial Democracy. *Economics Series II, Lecture No. 1,* Chicago, University of Chicago Press.

National Resources Board (as Member of the Board), *A Report on National Planning and Public Works in Relation to Natural Resources and Including Land Use and Water Resources, with Findings and Recommendations,* Government Printing Office.

Economic Reconstruction: Report of the Columbia University Commission, with others, New York, Columbia University Press.

National Planning Board, with Frederic A. Delano and Charles E. Merriam, *Final Report—1933–34,* Government Printing Office.

"The International Pattern in Business Cycles," in *XXII° Session de l'Institut International de Statistique, Londres, 1934,* The Hague.

1935

"The Social Sciences and National Planning," *Science,* Jan. 18, pp. 55–62.

"The National Bureau's Measures of Cyclical Behavior," with Arthur F. Burns, *Bulletin 57,* National Bureau of Economic Research.

"Commons on Institutional Economics," *American Economic Review,* Dec., pp. 635–652.

1936

"Production during the American Business Cycle of 1927–1933," with Arthur F. Burns, *Bulletin 61,* National Bureau of Economic Research.

"Intelligence and the Guidance of Economic Evolution," *Scientific Monthly,* Nov., pp. 450–465.

What Veblen Taught, Selected Writings of Thorstein Veblen, edited with an Introduction by Wesley C. Mitchell, New York, Viking Press.

1937

The Backward Art of Spending Money and Other Essays,
New York, McGraw-Hill Book Co.

1938

"Statistical Indicators of Cyclical Revivals," with Arthur F.
Burns, *Bulletin 69,* National Bureau of Economic Research.

1939

"Science and the State of Mind," *Science,* Jan. 6, pp. 1–4.
"In Memoriam: Edwin R. A. Seligman," *Political Science
Quarterly,* Sept., 3 unnumbered pages following p. 480.
"The Public Relations of Science," *Science,* Dec. 29, pp. 599–
607.
"Edwin Robert Anderson Seligman: 1861–1939," *American
Economic Review,* Dec., pp. 911–913.

1940

"Feeling and Thinking in Scientific Work," *Social Science,*
July, pp. 229–232.

1941

"J. Laurence Laughlin," *Journal of Political Economy,* Dec.,
pp. 875–881.
"Conservation, Liberty and Economics," in *The Foundations
of Conservation Education,* edited by the Committee on
Conservation Education of the National Wildlife Federation, Washington, The Federation, pp. 1–12.
"Economic Resources and Their Employment," in *Studies in
Economics and Industrial Relations,* Philadelphia, University of Pennsylvania Press, pp. 1–23.

1942

Abstract of an address, "The Effects of the Civil War on
Prices, Wages, and the Distribution of Income," *American
Economic Review,* March, Supplement, pp. 228–229.
"Annual Report of the President of the Academy of Political
Science," *Political Science Quarterly,* March, pp. 1–6.

"National Unity and Individual Liberties," *School and Society*, June 13, pp. 653–660.

1943

"Wartime 'Prosperity' and the Future," *Twenty-third Annual Report of the Director of Research* (published as *Occasional Paper 9*), March, National Bureau of Economic Research.

1944

"Economics in a Unified World," *Social Research*, Feb., pp. 1–10.

A discussion of "Political Science, Political Economy, and Values," papers by Arthur Salz and Herbert von Beckerath, *American Economic Review*, March, Supplement, pp. 48–50.

Contribution to "Symposium by Past Presidents of the American Economic Association on the Topic: What Should Be the Relative Spheres of Private Business and Government in Our Postwar American Economy?" *American Economic Review*, March, Supplement, pp. 292–294.

"Facts and Values in Economics," *Journal of Philosophy*, April 13, pp. 212–219.

"Prices and the Cost of Living in Wartime," with Simon Kuznets and Margaret G. Reid, Report of the Technical Committee, June 15, published in *Report of the President's Committee on the Cost of Living*, Government Printing Office, 1945, pp. 243–369.

Four articles on the postwar economic situation, *New York Times.* "Depression-Proof Economy Is Sought," Sept. 18, p. 22; "Inflation Threat Seen with Peace," Sept. 19, p. 28; "Wage Unrest Seen Following Peace," Sept. 20, p. 29; "U. S. Faces Problem as World Creditor," Sept. 21, p. 27.

"The Role of Money in Economic History," *Journal of Economic History*, Supplement IV, Dec., pp. 61–67.

1945

Testimony before a Subcommittee of the Committee on Military Affairs, October 29. In *Hearings on Science Legislation*,

Senate Committee on Military Affairs, 79th Congress, 1st Session, Part 4 (Oct. 29–Nov. 1, 1945) , pp. 738–744, 775–776, 781–782, 784–786.

1946

"Empirical Research and the Development of Economic Science," in *Economic Research and the Development of Economic Science and Public Policy*, National Bureau of Economic Research, pp. 3–20.

Measuring Business Cycles, with Arthur F. Burns, National Bureau of Economic Research.

1947

"The Role of Research in Economic Progress," in *The Conditions of Industrial Progress*, Industrial Research Department, Wharton School of Finance and Commerce, University of Pennsylvania, pp. 52–61.

"Irving Fisher (1867–1947)," in *Year Book of the American Philosophical Society*, pp. 243–246.

1949

Lecture Notes on Types of Economic Theory, 2 vols., New York, Augustus M. Kelley.

1951

What Happens during Business Cycles: A Progress Report, edited with an Introduction by Arthur F. Burns, National Bureau of Economic Research.